Tomatoes for Everyone

CW01019576

Other books by Allen Gilbert:

Dreaming of Roses
No Garbage: Composting and Recycling
Yates Organic Guide to Bulbs
Yates Green Guide to Gardening
The Natural Gardener (Vegetable chapter)
Yates Guide to Trees and Shrubs

Tomatoes
for Everyone
A Practical Guide to Growing
Tomatoes All Year Round

Allen Gilbert

HYLAND HOUSE

First published in Australia in 1997 by
Hyland House Publishing Pty Ltd
Hyland House
387-389 Clarendon Street
South Melbourne
Victoria 3205

© text and photographs Allen Gilbert 1997

This book is copyright. Apart from any fair dealing for the
purposes of private study, research, criticism or review, as
permitted under the Copyright Act, no part may be reproduced
by any process without written permission. Enquiries should be
addressed to the publisher.

National Library of Australia
Cataloguing-in-publication data:

Gilbert, Allen.
    Tomatoes for everyone: a practical guide to growing
    tomatoes all year round.

    Bibliography.
    Includes index.
    ISBN 1 86447 019 4.

    1. Tomatoes. I. Title.

635.642

Typeset in Australia by Solo Typesetting, South Australia
Printed in Singapore by Toppan Printing Co. Ltd.

Contents

Acknowledgements

I would like to thank many people, but in particular those people who looked at the original disorganised first draft of this book: Clive Blazey and Will Ashburner of Digger's Seeds, Dick Wall and James Wall of Walls Floriana, Jude and Michael Fanton of the Seed Savers' Network and Judy Horton from Yates. Also thanks to Ian Pascoe for checking the scientific names of diseases that are included in this book.

Hundreds of gardeners have contributed to the information in the book, including people who have shown and/or discussed ideas with me over the years and all those gardeners that helped with experimental field trials with tomato plants. There are lots of great gardeners that have given secret formulas or personal systems and methods for growing tomatoes that are included in the text and many home cookery experts have given family recipes. Among those I would like to personally thank are Phyllis Angell, Tony Baker, Peter Bennett, Richard Body, Laurie Cosgrove, Ruth Cosgrove, Dulcie Culph, Esther Deans, Elizabeth Dudley, Jack Eagan, George Edson, Isobel Gilbert, Mrs Goldsmith, Marge Hancock, Ken Hawkey, Elizabeth Jenkins, Margaret Keuris, Alan and Doreen Kingsbury. Tim and Morag Loh, Dorothy Manning, Alma Mehan, Mary O. Michaux, Jim Moore, Iris Purnell, Jack Rae, Irene Sinclair, John Small, Errol Stewart, Vera Storer, Pat Taylor and Theo.

Last but not least thanks to the editorial gang at Hyland House especially Rose Kitching and Anne Godden who organised the draft into something readable and to Al Knight for the superb design work.

Introduction

The tomato is native to South America and was brought to Europe by the first explorers. At first it was grown in gardens as a decorative ornamental plant and was thought to be an aphrodisiac. Sometimes the fruit was eaten but only after it had been cooked. Tomatoes were never eaten raw because they were thought to be poisonous.

Records on the planting and use of the tomato plant differ, but by the early 1800s the plant was being grown in gardens in many countries as a vegetable. The English seed company Sutton and Sons, in their book *The Culture of Vegetables and Flowers from Seeds and Roots* (1884), has this to say about the tomato:

The Tomato of late years attained to some degree of the appreciation it deserves, and amongst the more talented and spirited of English gardeners, it has become a representative of the fine arts department of utilitarian horticulture. It is, we believe, destined to increased and increasing importance, and we hope the day is not distant when every

Tomatoes growing in the central Gobi desert area of China, showing the deep irrigation ditches that conserve moisture, the unique staking system and companion planting of beans.

garden will produce an abundance throughout a great proportion of the year of its handsome, wholesome, and delicious fruits. When the refreshing, appetising, and corrective properties of Tomato soup become generally known, the cultivation of this noble fruit will progress by leaps and bounds, although at present time the interest taken in the crop is great and ever augmenting.

By the end of the eighteenth century, commercial cropping had begun in the United Kingdom. In *The Gardener's Assistant*, vol. 1, edited by William Watson (1936), mention is made of the boom in tomato production and the money to be made by commercial growers. Growers made up to £200 per acre per season by growing tomatoes in the open

1

ground; this was a great deal of money in those times. Of course the prophecy of tomatoes growing in most home gardens has come true.

Tomato seed was introduced into Australia during the days of early settlement and some specific varieties that have been grown in Australia can be traced to American, Chinese, English, Greek, Italian, Lebanese and Russian immigrants.

Why a Book on Growing Tomatoes?

It's not surprising that tomatoes are the world's most popular vegetable for the home gardener. They are easy to grow, require very little room and the difference between a home-grown tomato and a shop-bought one has to be tasted to be believed. Shop-bought tomatoes often have tough skins and taste like wet cardboard. This is because they have been selected over the years for their ability to withstand mechanical harvesting techniques. They are resistant to bruising and can be picked while green for long storage, but aren't soft, juicy and delicious.

Home-grown tomatoes on the other hand are delicious! Home gardeners can choose flavour over productivity. They can obtain unusual or old varieties and there are literally *hundreds* of tomato varieties and cultivars to choose from:

- bush types that don't need to be pruned
- climbing vines for trellis frames or stakes
- varieties and cultivars ideal for pots

Their fruit can be:

- large to very small
- flattened, heart-shaped, globular, pear-shaped, round—or any variation on this
- red, pink, white, yellow, orange and greens, yellow or green striped, purple, black

and suitable for pureeing, bottling, drying, stuffing or just eating raw!

Tomatoes can be grown in a number of ways to suit your lifestyle. The traditional way is in raised garden beds, but the plants can also thrive in non-dig gardens, pots or hanging baskets and simple hydroponic systems. Even children can grow tomatoes using a grow-bag or a bale of hay, or they can germinate seeds in a simple greenhouse made from a recycled plastic bottle!

In temperate, warm and tropical zones tomatoes can be grown all year round. Elsewhere, homemade or commercially bought heating structures will extend their growing and cropping time. Gardeners living in tropical zones are limited only by the wet season, when humidity is extremely high. Even then though, the use of humidity-resistant cultivars, a covered area and a de-humidifier can still allow tomatoes to be grown all year round

There are many toxic fungicides and insecticides likely to be on conventionally farmed tomatoes. The fruit may also contain heavy metals such as cadmium in their tissue due to the use of non-organic fertilisers. Tomatoes are easy to adapt to organic growing techniques. By using correct watering techniques and crop rotation, growing companion plants and using registered organic pest and disease control methods and organic fertilisers, or choosing hardy cultivars, you can prevent the build-up of pests and diseases and have the benefit of chemical-free tomatoes. You can join organic gardening and farming

A selection of cultivars and varieties: Black Russian (black), Green Zebra (green), Tommy Toe (medium to small) Red Cherry (small red), Tigerella (red-yellow stripes), Amish Paste (elongated red).

organisations and read books on organic gardening, permaculture and self-sufficiency if you want to know more about the various techniques. The availability of grafted plants in nurseries, and the ease with which you can graft your own plants onto disease-resistant rootstocks, is making organic growing much easier and more profitable. One grafted plant may yield up to 35 kg (77 lb) of fruit or more during one season. A multi-grafted plant can produce several types of tomato.

Tomatoes are extremely versatile when used in cooking. The list of recipes that includes tomatoes is endless. They can be eaten fresh, sun dried, or in paste form to add flavour and colour to any number of recipes: salads, sauces, stews, soups, casseroles, pies — everything!

Tomatoes are good for you. They contain vitamins A and C and small amounts of other vitamins and minerals. They also protect against cancer. A report in the *Herald Sun* (7 December 1995) mentions research done by Dr Edward Giovannucci at Harvard University. His research provides statistical evidence connecting the eating of tomatoes and the incidence prostate cancer. Men eating tomatoes regularly have far less chance of contracting prostate cancer. Tomatoes can also be used as an immediate remedy for sunburn. Placing tomato juice on the burnt skin reduces the pain. (It is better, however, to cover up, wear a hat and avoid sunburn and the almost inevitable skin cancer.)

At this point you may be wondering why you need a book to help you grow these trouble-free, tasty, healthy plants. You may be able to grow the same old Grosse Lisse seedlings bought from the nursery year after year, but for the connoisseur gardener and cook who wishes to try their wings on the enormous variety of subtle tastes and uses available in the thousand and one cultivars and varieties of tomato, wishes to extend the growing season so that they may enjoy ripe tomatoes all the year round, and wishes to expand their knowledge of organic gardening techniques — this book is not just an option, it is a necessity.

1   Growing Tomatoes

Richard Body's superb
two-week-old tomato
seedlings, grown in his
special mix (cow manure,
rice hulls and chicken
manure).

1.1 Growing from Seed

It is usually assumed that tomato seeds can be sown only at certain fixed times of the year, depending on where you live. However, they can be sown into pots or trays *at any time* using the heating structures described in chapter 3.4—even winter. If the seeds are sown in late winter/early spring, the seedlings can be planted out when the warm weather arrives, and ripe fruit can be obtained by late spring. Without using heating structures most gardeners living in cool to temperate climates think they are lucky to have ripening tomatoes by midsummer! If you are in an area that receives heavy snowfall during winter and early spring, a protective heated greenhouse is necessary to grow plants and extra lighting may also be needed.

New Ideas about when to Sow

Many gardeners sow two to five seeds in the one 15 cm (6 in) pot, just to make sure they get one plant to germinate; usually the strongest seedling is kept and the others cut off or gently pulled up. Don't sow the seeds too deep or they may not germinate. Just lightly cover them with seed-raising mix. Don't sow the seeds too close together if you can help it. Ideally they should be about 2½ cm (1 in) apart.

Sowing into Pots

All trays, pots and the tools used to propagate plants must be scrubbed to remove soil and plant material before use, and, preferably, sterilised. Household materials such as Dettol, bleach, phenol and methylated spirits are all suitable disinfectants. Bordeaux (available from nurseries) can be mixed into a thin slurry with water as an alternative.

Clean Pots and Trays

Once sown, the seed tray or pot needs to be placed in a warm environment (preferably about 20°C/68°F) and in a position which receives plenty of light. Small enclosed propagation kits, which can be readily opened for air flow once the seeds have germinated, or if the temperature is higher than 30°C (86°F) are ideal for raising seedlings (see p. 63). Another way to keep seeds warm is to use covered black-coloured pots, terracotta pots or metal containers, which absorb then radiate heat into the mix inside them.

Keeping the Seeds Warm

Heating Structures

JACK EAGAN'S SEED WARMING METHOD

Jack Eagan has been growing early-fruiting tomato plants for many years. For propagation Jack uses recycled polystyrene fruit boxes which retain heat. At the base of the box (with plenty of drainage holes in it) he places fresh grass clippings and, on top of that, a seed-raising mix (in this case mature compost), into which he sows the tomato seed. A pane of glass is placed over the top of the box. The heat provided by the composting green grass and the retained heat from the sun is sufficient to ensure good seed germination. This environment keeps the young tomato plants growing until they are ready to transplant into an open garden bed.

Organic Heating

TONY BAKER'S HEATED TRAYS

Mr Tony Baker invented this method for keeping seeds warm. He built a

This propagation box is fully enclosed, preventing the germinating seeds from drying out. Vents in the top allow some ventilation.

Jack Eagan's warming method is like a homemade propagation box. Both polystyrene and glass are easy to get hold of and provide instant warmth to seeds and young plants.

square-based, open-ended, black pyramid about 1 m (3 ft) tall. It was made from metal sheets but other heat-absorbing materials could also be used. Into this was placed a barrowful of grass clippings and one handful of compressed organic fertiliser pellets. The organic mix will soon start to compost and give off heat. Propagation trays can then be placed on top of the pyramid and free heat will be supplied to the base of the sown seed, ensuring quick germination. During cool weather the pyramid can be placed inside an igloo, greenhouse or sunroom.

Seed Mixes

One method of sowing seed: two or three seeds are planted into each compost-filled cup of an egg carton and soil is lightly sprinkled over them. As the seedlings grow, the paper carton breaks down and the roots grow into the soil.

Seed mixes must:
- ✺ be lightweight and crumbly
- ✺ be able to absorb and hold water
- ✺ contain *very small* amounts of a complete range of plant food, roughly about *one-sixth* of the amount of fertiliser needed for maturing or mature tomato plants
- ✺ drain well
- ✺ have a pH near neutral (pH 7)

A good natural organic seed mix for tomatoes is cow manure — it is lightweight and crumbly, it acts as a sponge and holds the water so that it is readily available for plants, it contains some nutrients, it drains well and is slightly acidic. I have used cow manure as an example just to explain the attributes of an ideal seed sowing mix.

There are many materials suitable for raising seeds and these can be used individually or in various proportions depending on their local availability. Most home gardeners make their mix using at least one from each of the following:
- ✺ **a humus-rich material to hold water** e.g. bagasse (sugar cane waste), compost, sandy loam, leaf mould, mulch, mushroom compost, palm peat (copra peat), sawdust—composted, sedge peat (from sedge plants), shredded seaweed, pasteurised soil, peat moss, tea leaves, water-absorbent granules, wood ash, worm castings
- ✺ **a granular product to give extra aeration** e.g. burnt rice hulls, coal dust, coke, crushed cotton seed husks, diatomite, fern fibre, foam

This mix contains recycled polystyrene, perlite and peat moss (about a third of each) and is ideal for tomatoes.

Tony Baker's heated propagation trays. All you need is a heat-absorbing material such as metal to build a pyramid and organic materials that will compost and create heat.

blocks, grape marc, perlite, peanut shells, pine bark, plastic chips/ granules, rice hulls, rock chips—very coarse, rock wool, sand, scoria, sunflower seed husks, vermiculite, wood charcoal, woollen waste, zeolites

☙ **a sprinkle of lime to supply calcium**
☙ **a *tiny* amount of granular or pelletised organic slow-release fertiliser** e.g. pelletised cow or fowl manure, rock dust, wood ash. Some gardeners just use rich compost as a seed mix without adding any extra nutrients

---

Seed and seedling mix which has been used for tomatoes before should never be recycled for growing tomato seeds again; use it on the garden or for potted plants.

Mixes You Can Try

Experiment with mixes and choose one that works for you. The following mixes are not all as good as each other in terms of the factors mentioned earlier, but the suggestions will, I hope, give some encouragement and reassure you when preparing your own seed-raising mix. Lime and a little slow-release fertiliser can be added to any of the following mixes.

compost 100%
compost 100% plus urine (10% solution) every watering
compost 50%, sand 50%
cow manure 100%
cow manure 70%, sand 30%
composted pine bark, animal manure and sandy loam (33% of each)
peat moss 100%
palm peat 100%
peat moss 50%, sandy loam, 50%
peat moss, sand, compost (33% of each)
pure sand 100%
polystyrene pieces, peat moss, river sand, finely graded bark chips
    (25% of each)

sandy loam 10–30%, compost or composted manure 70–90%

worm castings 100% (well drained)

worm castings 80%, shredded paper 10%, plus composted organic fertiliser 10%

RICHARD BODY'S MUCK AND MAGIC MIX

I met Richard Body at the Royal Melbourne Show several years ago. He had a tray of the best grown tomato plants I had ever seen. The special mix used by Richard is a very simple organic one that has taken years to perfect. He has allowed me to convey this secret mix to you. Use about 50 per cent of **composted cow manure** and 50 per cent of a 50:50 ratio composted mix of **rice hulls** and **chicken manure**. Plant the seeds in shallow flats, propagating units, trays or containers and keep the containers warm. Seedlings are up and ready to transplant within two weeks. For gardeners who will be transplanting the seedlings into heavy soils, an addition to the above mix of about 10 to 20 per cent **washed river sand** is recommended.

MUSHROOM MIX HAS TOO MUCH SALT

I tried growing tomato seedlings in a plastic bag of spent mushroom mix collected from the processing factory. The tomato plants grew and produced fruit but, because the mix had a high salt content, they did not really flourish. That they grew at all shows the hardiness of tomato crops. I believe that in some countries such as Israel, scientists have developed salt-resistant tomato plants for use where only saline water from bore water supplies is available for irrigation.

Some mushroom growers produce spent composted materials with low salt readings that *are* suitable for growing tomato seedlings, but they are better used in a mix. A mixture of **mushroom compost, composted animal manure** and **sand** is ideal for pot-grown plants. Extra nutrient will need to be added as the plants grow.

Here a plant is growing and producing fruit while planted in mushroom compost. The high pH and high salt content of some mixes are not ideal for tomatoes.

Cleaning the Seed Mix

The organisms that can cause damping off disease are present in most garden soils. This is why many gardeners do not use natural garden soil in any of their potting or seedling mixes. Mixes using compost, worm castings and materials not prepackaged may have to be sterilised to prevent these diseases occurring. Heating to 60°C (140°F) for 30 minutes in an oven or microwaving the tray and contents will achieve this.

USING THE SUN

Another way to pasteurise the seedling mix is by using the sun.

1   Place the mix in a clear plastic bag, seal the bag and flatten it out to 10 cm (4 in) depth.

2   Place the bag in direct sunlight for a few days, turning it every day. Inside it will become very hot (temperatures may reach in excess of 100°C/212°F) and this will kill weed seeds and any harmful disease organisms.

Sowing into the Ground

Tomato seeds can be planted out into the open ground as soon as the soil warms up to about 20°C (68°F). In cooler regions this is usually late spring and in warmer regions at any time of the year. Warming the soil using structures such as the Hydronurture igloo (see p. 63) will enable early outdoor seed sowing.

Mrs Goldsmith, a home gardener, has a unique system of growing tomato seeds that will not suit gardeners who are fussy and particular, but it will suit those who like things easy. The one condition necessary for success is that the soil where the tomatoes are to be grown must be well drained, unpolluted, loose, friable and contain plenty of organic matter (see p. 13 Preparing Garden Beds).

The Easiest Way in the World—Put on Your Hobnailed Boots!

The method is to put on your hobnailed boots and just squash and grind a healthy red tomato fruit into the soil where you want the plants to grow. This is usually done at harvest time. The seeds squashed from the fruit will lie dormant while the soil is cold and germinate when it warms up. This method has been used in one tomato plot for several years running and is still producing results without the build-up of any diseases. However, to be on the safe side crop rotation is the best bet and choosing a new spot each year to squash your tomato is a good idea.

There are lots of structures you can use to protect seeds and seedlings from cold weather when they are planted straight into the garden, either homemade or shop-bought. They are described on pp. 60−67.

Keeping the Soil Warm

Heating Structures

COMPOST ROOT WARMER

Organic Heating

One of the earliest recorded ways of keeping plants' roots warm is by utilising the heating qualities of animal manure. Thick layers of fresh green manure (20 to 30 cm/8 to 12 in) can be placed in trenches under the topsoil of garden beds where temperature-sensitive seeds such as tomatoes are to be planted. The heat generated by the composting material radiates upwards, warming the topsoil and the roots of the plants. The warmth provided by composting manure inside can also be used to heat the immediate environment in a greenhouse.

The heating structures described in chapter 3.4 can be combined with the above organic methods to provide maximum protection from cold and frost.

Some gardeners use water-absorbent powders and crystals (available from nurseries) to help sow seeds. The powder or crystals are mixed with water and, as they absorb the water, they thicken to a gel. The seed is stirred into the gel. It is easiest if the mixing can be done in a plastic bag and once the gel has thickened and the seed is evenly distributed, one corner of the bag can be cut away and the contents squeezed out (like toothpaste) in a line along the garden bed or into seed trays, and a light covering of soil placed over it. The mix can be placed in a warm environment for a few days to pre-germinate the seed or the seed can be sown soon after the gel mix is prepared.

Seed-sowing Jelly

This method ensures the seed is planted evenly, prevents oversowing, conserves moisture and provides the seed with a reservoir of water.

In the first few weeks the young seedlings can be attacked by diseases, such as pythium, that cause damping off (rotting of the stem near the soil) or grey furry fungal growth (botrytis) on the stems, which will

General Care

Seeds evenly distributed in gel and ready to sow. Use a pliable plastic bag so that one corner of the bag can be cut open, allowing the seed to be squirted along the row just like toothpaste (see previous page).

Tomato seedlings showing elongated growth due to lack of light. Some of these seedlings were attacked by diseases such as damping off, perhaps because this homemade seedling box is not easy to sterilise.

quickly kill them. Other fungus or bacteria can also be a problem where seedlings are too close together, preventing adequate air flow.

Collecting and Storing Your Own Seed

Many home gardeners and organic growers are interested in preserving heritage plants and, therefore, try to save their own seed. Saving seed is particularly important with tomato plants because hundreds of old cultivars have completely disappeared and hundreds more are no longer commercially available. They only survive because of the seed savers' networks around the world. Gardeners can save their own seed and share it within seed savers' network organisations (see pp. 103 and 131–132).

If you want to collect and store your own tomato seed, the selection of the fruit is very important. Seed should be taken from uniformly shaped, ripe fruit that has come from plants with no disease symptoms such as bacterial speck, bacterial wilt or virus infections. A tomato fruit or seed given to you by a fellow gardener may be infected with a disease that can be transferred in or on the seed. Seed fermentation, hot water treatment or sodium hypochlorite (see below) can be used to rid the seed of any diseases. Remember that seed saved from named hybrid forms (crosses made by plant breeders) may not produce plants exactly the same as the parent plant but non-hybrid (open-pollinated) forms will reproduce true to form.

Collecting

Tomato seed can easily be collected by home gardeners.
1   Select a ripe fruit and spoon out the seed from the fruit seed cavities into a small kitchen strainer.

Collecting seed is easy using a kitchen strainer.

When saving tomato seed, clean it first, then place it onto absorbent paper towelling in neat rows so that when it dries and sticks to the paper it can be cut into ready-to plant strips.

2   Place the strainer containing the pulp under running water and press against the pulp with a spoon to force it through the strainer mesh. The seed will be left behind.

If you want to collect and clean the seed at the same time, use the method described under Fermentation.

Cleaning

Cleaning the seed is generally a good idea. It will enhance germination, improve seed storage time and rid the seed of flesh which may contain disease organisms. There are three main ways of getting rid of diseases. The method used will depend on the disease you are trying to get rid of (see chapter 4.2). If you just want to make sure your seed is clean, any of the methods can be used.

FERMENTATION
This process will clean the seed and get rid of some of the seed-borne diseases at the same time.
1   Select very ripe tomato fruit and place them in an open container, squashing them as you do so. This sets off the natural rotting and fermentation of the fruit. During fermentation, bacteria and fungi use the tomato flesh as a food source and eat it until there is no flesh left sticking to the individual seeds. This can take one week or more. The fermenting seed mix must not be left too long or the seeds may start to germinate due to the warmth given off during the process.
2   Remove the floating seeds from the rotting mess and wash them.
3   Dry the seeds.

HOT WATER TREATMENT
Some seed-borne diseases can only be eliminated by a controlled-temperature hot water treatment. All you need is a frying pan, boiling water and a good thermometer. A constant temperature of 54°C (130°F)

for half an hour is recommended to kill pathogens; this temperature will not destroy the seeds. They can then be dried.

SODIUM HYPOCHLORITE TREATMENT

Another method of cleaning seed is to soak it in a water and sodium hypochlorite mix for a few minutes. Tomato seeds treated in this way must be washed in clean water prior to sowing.

Drying

To dry the seed, place it on some hard or slippery material, such as greaseproof paper, a teflon-coated surface, china plate, or oven tray, and place in the sun. Alternatively, put it on blotting paper or absorbent paper towelling in neat lines and when the seed is dry the paper can be cut into ready-to-plant strips.

Storing

The collected seeds can be stored in an open paper bag or a sealed jam jar or wrapped in tin foil and placed in a dry, airy, cool storage place to ensure they remain fertile. Packets of silica can be placed in the jar with the stored seed. Silica powder absorbs moisture from the air and can be used to dry seed to about a 5 per cent moisture level. It is possible to store tomato seed for up to seven years and still not lose viability.

If the stored seed is subjected to too much temperature variation, or too much moisture, it may dry out, pre-germinate or gradually lose viability and will not grow when sown. This often happens if you take the stored seed out to plant some of it and don't reseal the container immediately.

Commercial seed companies now package seed in sealed silver sachets for longer storage life.

1.2 Growing from Seedlings

Hardening Off

Before you transplant the seedlings from the seed trays or pot, you need to harden them off. Take them out of the warm protected environment in which they germinated and place them in 40 to 50 per cent shade for a few days.

Transplanting

Wait until the young seedlings have begun to grow their second lot of true leaves before transplanting them into individual 1 L (¼ gallon) pots or the garden bed. What look like the plant's first 'leaves' are actually cotyledons (part of the seed) and not true leaves. Ideally the seedlings should be about 5 cm (2 in) high at the time of transplanting.

Cut the closely grown seedlings out of the seed trays or pots with a block of soil around their root systems, then transplant them into 1 L (¼ gallon) pots or directly into garden beds. When transplanting, make sure you handle the plants with great care. Grip them by their leaves and do not touch the stem as this is usually very tender and can become bruised. Bruising may inhibit growth and cause fungi or bacteria to attack the injury point. Space individual plants 30 to 45 cm (12 to 18 in) apart in garden beds.

If you have tall-growing varieties that will need to be staked put your stakes in when you transplant so you don't disturb the plant roots later (see p. 15).

Tomato plants prefer the maximum amount of sunlight possible and shelter from wind and frost. Continuous growth and fruit set can only be achieved if the temperature does not drop below 21°C (70°F), but even warmer temperatures are preferred. Plants require good air movement in and between one another and between the leaves to prevent the build-up of disease. They must be grown in well drained humus-rich soils or potting mix, and be supplied with plenty of water.

General Requirements

Many gardeners believe that digging loads of animal manure into their soil at a rate of one barrow load per square metre of row is all that is needed to produce healthy tomatoes. Usually, the manure should be dug in two to three months before planting the seedlings. This will allow it to break down; the soil microbe activity will increase, which will be beneficial to the tomato seedlings. If seedlings are to be planted into beds containing high rates of *fresh* manure, they may burn unless a layer of compost or soil (1 to 5 cm/½ to 2 in thick) is placed directly above it.

Preparing Garden Beds

When preparing garden beds or pots for tomatoes, it is important to add calcium. Calcium is needed to strengthen the cell walls of the tomato plant and its fruit. Its presence will prevent blossom end rot developing on the fruit and may help with general disease prevention. Blossom end rot shows as a scaly sunken patch (which often turns black) at the base of tomato fruits (see below and p. 17). To supply calcium:
☙ Sprinkle garden lime at a rate of one handful per square metre (this rate may be increased with very acid soils).

Strengthen Plants with Calcium

A transplanted seedling showing its third and fourth set of true leaves. Plants can be transplanted any time after they have developed their second set of true leaves. The yellowing of the foliage indicates that it was not hardened off before transplanting.

Blossom end rot, causing a distinct browning or blackening of the basal end of the fruits. This is caused by a number of factors including infrequent watering, hot weather and lack of calcium.

☙ With alkaline soils (to test this use a simple pH test kit) the application of lime would make the soils too alkaline, so use ground-dug gypsum instead. The use of gypsum from industrial sources is not recommended because it has a talc-like consistency and is highly alkaline.

The Sting: Recipe for Healthy Tomatoes

Give your tomato plants a real sting using dried, powdered stinging nettle leaves. When placed at the bottom of the planting hole, the dried material will increase biological activity within the soil and improve plant health and resistance to disease. The dried leaves can also be placed in a bucket, to which water is added to allow the mixture to ferment. The fermented water, which contains silicon, is sprayed onto the foliage of the tomato plants and is effective in deterring insect attacks, improving the health of the plants and increasing the ability of the plant to absorb sunlight. Stinging nettle preparations are readily available to home gardeners in Europe and Australian gardeners can prepare their own dried nettle leaves using stinging nettles picked from the garden.

Seedling Mixes

If you plant your seedlings straight into the garden bed, you won't need a seedling mix. If, however, you think they're not ready to be planted out or you don't have a garden bed, you will need to put them in a larger pot and get rid of all the old seed mix.

The main difference between the mix used for seeds and that used for seedlings is the level of fertiliser or food added. Seeds need virtually none because they aren't growing, just germinating using stored food in the seed. The more growth that is occurring, the more fertiliser must be added. Any of the mixes recommended on page 7 for seeds can be used for seedlings but extra fertiliser, either slow release or liquid, will need to be added. If you plan to grow your tomatoes completely in pots, see chapter 2.2 for year-round hints.

Ways to Plant

Bury the Stem Deeply

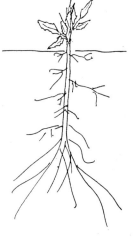

Tomato plants, unlike most other plant species, will respond well if you bury the stem of the plant as long as some foliage is left above ground. The tomato will grow extra roots from the buried stem and will not get stem or collar rot *provided the soil is well drained.* Some gardeners bury the plants to the first set of leaves, others bury three-quarters of the plant and leave only the topmost leaves showing. Leaves that may be buried at planting should be removed beforehand. Some gardeners bury the plant at an angle or lie it horizontally along the garden bed, burying the whole stem and turning the topmost shoot upwards. Drenching the buried stem area with a liquid seaweed product after planting will initiate even more fibrous roots. Extra roots give extra production and healthier plants.

Lie Them Down

Sometimes tomato plant stems flop down and form roots where they touch the soil or mulch material. Mr Ken Hawkey, observing this, suggests that maybe we are growing tomatoes the wrong way and should utilise their ability to self-root by deliberately training them to loop in and out of the soil causing the plant to spread out rather than grow upwards on stakes. Ken has observed that the stem growth from the areas where the tomato has layered produced a better crop of tomatoes than the parts of the plant that were staked and no pruning was necessary! Try it! It may work for you too.

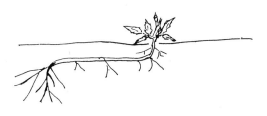

Washed River Gravel

One system developed by a Lebanese-born Australian gardener is to heap washed river gravel above ground all around the base of the tomato plants, covering the stems to about 15 to 25 cm (6 to 10 in). The cropping results are phenomenal compared to tomatoes grown in the usual way.

General Care

Staking Plants

There are several ways to support strong-growing tomato plants. One way is to use 2 m (6 ft) stakes and tie the tomato shoots to the stakes as they grow with cloth material, old stockings or pantyhose. This material is soft and stretchy and will not harm or cut the tomato plant stems but string or soft rope can also be used. If you want to stake your tomatoes, *put the stake in before you plant so that you don't damage the plant's roots*.

Tomato plants in a ringed wire support frame with companion plants (herbs including nasturtium).

Many new gardeners prefer not to stake their plants or use alternatives support systems such as the following:

- Groups of teepee-shaped stakes, bamboo poles or selected prunings can be stuck into the ground to form interesting shapes for plant support.
- Wire mesh can be rolled up into an open tube, which is supported between two posts. This can be placed over the plant for use as a climbing frame or set at an oblique angle for general support.
- Wires tightly strung between posts can be used to support the plants or to train a tomato as an espalier (this will also help pollination, see p. 17).
- Plastic webbing, wire mesh cages, or netting can be made into support frames.
- Some gardeners allow their tomatoes to sprawl naturally in among companion plants that help to hold the fruit off the ground.

Keeping Warm

Young seedlings will need protection when grown in areas subject to cold weather. Cold nights or freezing winds (temperatures below 21°C/ 70°F) will impede tomato plant growth. See chapter 3.4 for structures that can be used to keep seedlings warm.

Protection from Wind

Gardeners in dry and arid or windy regions may have to erect windbreaks around the garden. Aboriginal gardeners working gardens in the wind-swept Ceduna, South Australia, used hessian barriers to protect their gardens from severe winds and dust. Other kinds of wind-protecting barriers can be constructed using fencing materials, plastic webbing or by planting small shrubs. Food-producing climbing plants, such as beans, choko, pumpkins and kiwi fruit, planted around the edge of the tomato patch will also provide wind protection. Corn plants also provide excellent wind protection.

Feeding

The seedlings will need some kind of fertiliser as they grow — either slow-release granular fertilisers or organic liquid fertilisers, such as manure tea or liquid seaweed. Liquid fertilisers can be applied weekly or daily. Tomato plants are particularly sensitive to oversupply or undersupply of nutrients, and will show this in the way they grow. Thin, weedy plants indicate undernourishment (or lack of light); stocky dark green plants show an unbalanced food supply, and plants with yellow leaves show lack of nitrogen. Plants in the open ground are less likely to need extra feeding. See chapter 3.1 for information on organic fertilisers.

Here, roofing iron is being used as a windbreak. The iron also absorbs heat during the day and radiates it around the plants at night.

PROMOTE FLOWERING WITH POTASH

Potash in necessary to promote growth and flowering. It is sold in packets labelled sulphate of potash, muriate of potash or included in mixed fertiliser preparations. It can also be obtained from wood ash (see p. 50).

Irregular watering contibutes to the formation of blossom end rot (see p. 13), so water regularly (see pp. 57–60). Mulch your tomato plants early in summer with materials such as grass to reduce the amount of water needed and improve the structure of the soil (see chapter 3).

Watering and Mulching

Tomato plants must be pollinated in order to set fruit and we can't always rely on the bees, insects or the wind. To make sure that pollen is spread around the flowers some home gardeners train their tomato plants on string or wires that can be bumped or vibrated to release the pollen. Tomato plants, like many other fruiting plants, tend to keep producing fruit once the first fruit is formed, so inducing the plant to flower and then set fruit forces it into the fruiting habit to the benefit of the home gardener. Any small electronic vibrator device can be held against the flower cluster, main tomato stem or plant support frame to vibrate and shake pollen loose. Alternatively, a small fine-haired brush is sometimes used to poke into each flower in turn as a method of pollen transfer. The best time to pollinate is in the early morning when the flowers are open, rigid and turgid.

Pollinating for Fruit Set

Some gardeners have, by accident or neglect, found ways to get tomato plants to flower early. Both of the following methods involve depriving the plant for a period of time until the fruit sets and then returning conditions to normal.

STARVING

Grow seedlings in small pots in a warm place until they reach about 30 cm (12 in). The plants become potbound and are then starved and given minimum water. This causes them to respond as if they are going to die, so they begin to flower. The flowers are pollinated and as soon as some fruit has set, the plant is transferred to a larger pot or to the vegetable garden and normal feeding and watering is resumed.

CHILLING

Chill the small seedling plants for a short period before planting into bigger pots or the garden. The plant begins to flower soon after being planted out.

Promoting Early Flowers

Pruning has long been considered a must for tomatoes. It is a Victorian approach to gardening that we must keep everything neat and tidy and in its place. The heritage publication *The Gardener's Assistant*, revised by William Watson in 1936, says that tomatoes *have* to be pruned but warned against pruning too hard, thus hindering fruit production and

Pruning

Prune here

ripening. However, it doesn't make much difference to the crop whether you prune or not. Pruned plants may produce bigger fruits because there are fewer of them, but not necessarily, and the fruits produced on an unpruned plant are just as good. Recent field trials have shown that tomato plants left unpruned produce just as many or more tomatoes than those that are pruned. If you do prune, do it in late spring and midsummer.

The options are:

Tall-growing and Climbing Plants

- ☙ Prune so as to leave *two* to *five* main branches. Vigorous grafted tomatoes are often left with up to ten branches.
- ☙ Prune off the top part of the plant stem as it is growing so as to promote low multiple branching into a bush form. Once a bush is formed, stop pruning. This is my preferred option.
- ☙ Don't prune at all. This is a new approach for most gardeners but one worth trying! (See p. 15, Lie Them Down.)

All Plants

- ☙ Prune off the lower leaves to allow more light, improve air circulation and prevent the build-up of diseases.
- ☙ Don't prune at all.

Most gardeners prune by pinching off the lateral shoots with their fingernails; this reduces the foliage growing within the plant. It is best to pinch shoots at the tiny shoot growth stage.

USING PRUNING OFF-CUTS

Some gardeners use the laterals pinched from producing tomato plants at pruning time to grow new plants. They believe these plants produce better crops than the original plant. Try this as it will give you an extended tomato season, save you money and produce good crops.

Before. This shoot has been pruned and can be planted. It has been divided in two and some of the lower leaves have been removed.

After. Simply stick the cuttings into the soil and they will grow into new plants. Usually plants grown from cuttings will be more fruitful than the parent plant from which they were taken.

Before

After

1.3 Using Grafted Tomatoes

Grafting is the fitting together of two tomato plant pieces, one to provide the root system for the plant (usually the seedling rootstock) and the other, from another variety, to provide the cropping part of the plant (the scion). Grafted plants tend to give exceptional cropping and the plants grow much larger than they would on their own root system. Gardeners can expect up to 35+ kg (80 lb) of tomatoes from one grafted plant during one season.

Tomato plants usually grow so well from seed that home gardeners never think about grafting. However, recently there have been more and more incidents of crop failure due to a build-up of soil-borne or seed-borne diseases, making it more important to have grafted tomato plants that are disease resistant.

The advantage of grafting is that you can combine the disease-resistant roots of one plant with the delicious fruit of one or several others and have the best of both worlds! The grafted plants can be grown in a pot with an accompanying trellis, in a hanging basket, against a fence, or over a trellis structure to save space. They will provide a fruit salad bowl of tomatoes with different colours, sizes shapes and tastes from the garden.

You can graft more than one tomato variety onto the one plant, or several seedling tomatoes can be planted together in one pot, then all individually grafted. This would give you a succession of ripening tomato varieties spread over a longer cropping period.

Christian Pitsounis standing beside a plant which has both tomato and eggplant scions attached using cleft and bark grafts. The grafts are protected by plastic bags.

Many home gardeners think that grafting tomatoes is a job much too difficult for them or that it must be done by experts or people with a degree in botany. This is not true. Any home gardener can graft and have fun doing it. All you need is:

- a sharp knife
- a peg
- a dressmaker's pin
- budding tape or tying material
- a small plastic bag
- water
- tape
- a warm spot or a heating structure to shelter the plant (see pp. 60–67)

Hints for Growing Grafted Plants

Choosing a Rootstock

You don't need a tasty cultivar to use as a rootstock. Plants for rootstocks are chosen because they are hardy, vigorous, cold tolerant, disease resistant or provide a good fibrous root system. Selected 'wild' type cherry tomatoes with a vigorous growth habit and disease resistance are often used as rootstocks for grafting disease-susceptible and weak-growing cultivars onto. Seed for growing rootstock material is available from some seed companies.

Securing any Graft

When two pieces of plant are joined to form a graft, the joined area needs to be held tightly together to allow the pieces to grow together. Several materials can be used to achieve this:

- budding tape
- clothes pegs
- cotton
- dental floss
- hair clips
- miniature grafting pegs
- parafilm
- raffia
- rubber bands
- soft florist's tape
- string

Plastic Bag Around Graft

A narrow open-ended plastic bag with a few droplets of water (or water mixed with a liquid seaweed product) clinging to the inside of the bag, should be inserted over the graft once it has been secured. The plastic tent can be held in place with a small dressmaker's pin, pinned into the stem of the plant below the graft area. The bag should remain over the graft until the graft piece has started to grow, and can then be removed.

Methods of Grafting

Approach Graft

1   Grow a rootstock plant and a named cultivar side by side.
2   When the seedlings are 5 to 10 cm (2 to 4 in) tall they can be pulled together.
3   Cut a small slice of bark tissue from each stem where they touch.
4   Tie the stems together; where the stems contact each other they will form a graft.

5 Put a moistened plastic bag over the graft (see earlier).
6 Remove the *leafy part* of the rootstock and the *root system* of the scion when the graft has knitted. This leaves the tasty cultivar growing on top of the strong rootstock.

   Some nurseries sell approach-grafted plants with both root systems still attached. This is acceptable where no diseases are present or if both root systems are resistant to diseases. But if the tasty cultivar is susceptible to diseases such as fungal or bacterial root rot, the whole plant could become infected through one root system. It is better, therefore, to remove the root system of the tasty cultivar.

A graft held in place with thin pieces of budding tape and protected with a moisturised plastic bag, which is removed as soon as the graft starts to grow actively.

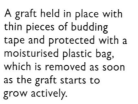

Tomato grafts can be held in place by tiny pegs that are removed as soon as the graft has knitted.

Bark grafts can be done on old or new stems.   *Bark Graft*
1 Cut the stem off the rootstock horizontally.
2 Make a slit into the bark tissue for about 2 cm (1 in) downwards.
3 Choose and cut a growing shoot from the tomato you want to grow (scion).
4 Re-cut the end of the shoot at an angle of about 30 degrees with a very sharp knife.
5 Remove all the leaves except the ones at the very tip of the cutting.
6 Force the scion down inside the bark (sloping side inwards) where the slit was made by lifting the bark gently and sliding the scion into place.
7 Secure the graft, put a moistened plastic bag over it (see earlier) and keep warm.
8 Remove the graft tape or peg when the graft has fully calloused and is strong.
9 Cut off any suckers that grow from beneath the graft area.

Because tomato plants have soft tissue stems they can easily be grafted   *Sloping Cut Graft*
using a simple 30-degree sloping cut on both the rootstock stem and the
scion. The cut sides are placed together and then held in place with
pins, tape, grafting pegs, hair clips or clothes pegs.

1 Make a downward sloping cut half to two-thirds of the way through   *Side Graft*
   the rootstock stem.

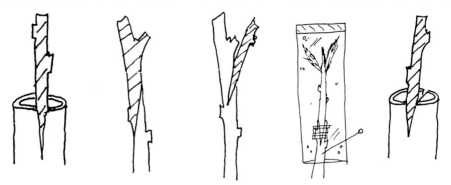

From left to right: bark graft, sloping cut graft, side graft, simple 'V' graft and cleft graft.

2   Prise the cut open.
3   Select a scion and cut a 'V' at its base.
4   Jam the scion into the cut on the rootstock.
5   Secure the graft and place a moistened plastic bag over it (see earlier).
6   When the graft has taken, remove the plastic bag and cut and remove the top leafy shoot of the rootstock.

The Simple 'V' Graft

1   Select a soft new shoot from the rootstock.
2   Cut it off horizontally.
3   Cut a 1 cm (½ in) slit into the cut stem.
4   Cut a growing shoot about 1 to 3 cm (½ to 1 in) long from the desired tomato cultivar (scion).
5   Remove the lower leaves and the top central growth (growing tip).
6   Cut the base of the shoot into a 'V' shape.
7   Insert the shoot into the cut in the rootstock, secure and cover with a moistened plastic bag (see earlier).
8   Remove the bag when the grafted piece starts vigorous new growth.

Cleft Graft

The cleft graft is just the same as the 'V' graft except that the cut is made into older stems or stems with a larger diameter.
1   Cut the stem of the plant to be used as the rootstock.
2   Slice into the cut stem and hold the gap open.
3   Prepare the scion as for the 'V' graft and insert it into the rootstock, placing it so the cambial layers touch. The cambial layer is the layer just under the bark tissue.
4   Cover with a moistened plastic bag (see earlier).
The cleft graft is not very successful when used on older tomato shoots because of the soft pithy tissue that develops in aged stems, but it is successful when used on soft new growth.

Multi-fruited Bush

EGGPLANTS AND TOMATOES
Some gardeners graft the eggplant, which is related to the tomato, onto tomato rootstocks to provide a more vigorous eggplant. Grafted eggplants can also be bought from plant nurseries. Various specific grafts are tried but the most common are 'V', approach and bark grafts.

RELATED SPECIES, TOMATOES AND EGGPLANTS

Using bark and 'V' grafts the author has grafted a tomato onto another related solanum plant species *Solanum orvum* (a weed originating from the West Indies). It has a prickly shrub-like stem so that the tomatoes themselves are elevated above the ground. Eggplants were grafted onto the same bush to provide a multi-cropping plant for the home garden.

Three Plants in One

Keen gardeners with limited space can grow a potted tomato plant with three different tomato cultivars grafted on it. All it takes is a bit of patience and some dexterity.

1 Take a small healthy seedling tomato plant for the rootstock.
2 Cut the top off so that the plant produces three or four new shoots.
3 Feed the plant well and keep it in a warm position or in a protected environment or greenhouse.
4 When the new shoots are 10 cm (4 in) long remove the tops.
5 Select three growing shoots from other tomato cultivars, perhaps from a neighbour's plants, and graft these onto the cut shoots.
6 Secure the graft piece in place and cover with a moist plastic bag (see earlier).
7 Keep the plant warm.

After the grafts have knitted each one will grow and produce its own type of fruit—all on the one plant!

Theo Pitsounis's grafted solanum plant under plastic cover showing good crops of both eggplant and tomatoes (a Greek heritage variety).

TOMATOES AND POTATOES

Tomatoes can also be grafted to potato so that both crops can be harvested from the one plant.

General Care of Grafted Plants

Grafted plants must be kept warm, protected from the wind and watered and mulched the same as seedlings (see pp. 15–17). They will also need to be pollinated once the flowers appear (see p. 17). The main difference in the kind of general care they need is when it comes to staking, feeding and pruning.

Staking

Grafted plants are great for espalier systems and can cover a large area — 1 to 2 m (3 to 6 ft) — each side of the main stem. If you use a trellis, don't use steel piping or copper materials for a trellis because the metal gets too hot and the copper may be toxic to the plants. When tying the plant, recycle old pantyhose or an old stocking.

Feeding

Fertilise grafted plants regularly as they have more growth and require more food than non-grafted plants.

Pruning

Grafted plants are usually grown on a trellis and need to have each main branch separate from the other to allow good air flow through the plant. Instead of leaving only one or two leaders when pruning, grafted plants can be left with six to ten leaders and still perform well. When pinching out side shoots, do this early to prevent large scarred areas that may be an entry point for pests or diseases.

Sucker Growth

Rootstock plants will sometimes throw up growths from the base under the graft union. If left unpruned, these suckers will grow strongly and take over, leaving the graft section weak and unhealthy. Three options are available to home growers:

1 Remove all sucker growth (probably desirable when eggplant has been grafted onto a tomato rootstock).
2 Continually pinch back sucker growth until the graft piece has developed into a strong healthy plant, then allow the rootstock section to grow and enable the production of two tomato types on the one plant.
3 Use the rootstock pieces to graft other tomato varieties onto so that gardeners have a multi-grafted plant with a number of tomato varieties on the one plant.

Before. This grafted plant is becoming thickened by shoot growth and is at the stage where pruning can be done to allow better air movement through the plant, reducing the incidence of diseases.

After. The same tomato plant has just been pruned, showing the amount of shoots that have been removed. Enough foliage must be left on the plant to protect it from sun and to allow it to manufacture sufficient food from sunlight through its leaves.

2 Ways to Grow

The children of St Arnaud state school placing the last layer of compost on a non-dig hay bale garden containing, straw, paper waste, animal manure, hay, lucerne and weeds.

2.1 Non-dig Gardens

In forests, non-dig organic gardens are the norm. Forest trees drop their leaves which contain nutrients that have been mined from the lower soil depths by the tree roots. The leaves mix with dead birds and animals, dust, insect droppings and animal droppings and form non-dig gardens composting on the soil surface. In these natural mulch gardens soil organisms break down all the organic components into forms of food that are readily taken up by plant roots and so the cycle continues.

Tomatoes love non-dig gardens and they seem to grow exceedingly well in any type of mulch or compost (see chapter 3).

Most non-dig gardens consist of layers of organic materials interspersed with liberal applications of organic fertilisers and then topped with a layer of material into which seedlings or seed can easily be planted. Soil, potting mix, peat moss, copra peat, worm castings or well-rotted compost can all be used for this. If the compost is weed free and is 1 to 5 cm (1 to 2 in) thick, weed growth under it will be suppressed and hardly any weeding will need to be done. To obtain weed-free, disease-free compost, gardeners must use the 'hot compost' method of composting (see p. 53). Almost any material of organic origin is suitable for non-dig gardens and gardens can either be multi-layered, using many materials, or built in a single layer using only one material.

The gardens can be built up high with or without boarded sides or just be piled on the surface of the soil. They can be inside the house, on concrete, on veranda areas, on old beds, in tyres, in drums, in pots or in portable above-ground beds. The garden shapes can be round, square, oblong, diamond, triangular or anything else! Large high non-dig gardens work best if you place pipes with holes in them (horizontally near the base or centre) through the garden to supply extra aeration to the centre of the unit and prevent the organic material from becoming too waterlogged. A small non-dig garden can be built and planted by one person in a very short time.

Types of Non-dig Gardens

Non-dig Compost Heap

The simplest non-dig garden is a discarded pile of compost. If you are lucky, tomato plant seeds in the compost waste will survive the composting process and grow, creating a natural non-dig garden. Seedling tomato plants originating from compost heaps seem more resilient and produce better root growth than their hybrid nursery-raised cousins.

Tomato plants will survive happily on the nutrients supplied by recycled garden and kitchen waste in the compost. If it has been well prepared and contains many different types of plant material, no extra nutrients will be needed, but better crops are usually obtained when extra organic nutrients are given to the plants after they start cropping (see pp. 45–50).

Esther Deans' Method: Layering Materials

Esther Deans introduced non-dig gardening to Australia in 1977. Her method of building a non-dig garden means that it requires minimal energy, less watering, no weeding and is easily managed. It consists of several layers in the following order:

- ✋ newspaper (as a base to suppress weeds)
- ✋ lucerne
- ✋ animal manure
- ✋ straw
- ✋ animal manure
- ✋ mature compost (a final layer into which to plant seeds or seedlings)

The straw and lucerne layers vary, but can be 10 to 30 cm (4 to 12 in) thick. Just *sprinkle* the manure on. The garden is watered as every layer is added and plants or seedlings planted as soon as it is finished. If the seedlings are watered in with one of the liquid seaweed products (see p. 48), their growth and survival will be greatly enhanced. (See *Esther Dean's Gardening Book: Growing Without Digging*.)

Council Mulch

Most city councils chip and shred organic waste obtained from the regular pruning of trees. This material is stockpiled and available to residents either free of charge, or at a very reduced price and can be bought by the truckload. If you hot compost the material before use, you will also get rid of weed seeds and any diseases (see p. 53). Mulch material gathered from old piles of compost can be recomposted by adding extra nitrogen and some moisture and thoroughly aerating the mix.

To make a non-dig garden from council mulch:

1 Spread wetted newspaper over the proposed garden area as a weed barrier.
2 Dump the composted council mulch on top of the newspaper.
3 Add some animal manure and a sprinkle of lime.
4 Turn the mulch a few times over a period of three to four weeks before you begin planting.
5 Plant tomato seedlings into the composting mulch and add a small handful of blood and bone on the area where each seedling is planted.
6 Apply liquid seaweed to the foliage and soil (as a drench) every two weeks during the growing season.

These bushes will survive and grow a medium crop of very large tomatoes.

COMMUNITY GARDENS

Gardeners with plots in community gardens should take advantage of the availability of shredded and compostable materials and set up giant non-dig gardens. Depending on supply, it may be possible to completely cover large areas with the shredded or chipped material, adding some chicken manure. The first plants in the prepared area serve to prepare the soil, build up biological activity, reduce weed populations and increase worm populations. Then the garden can be divided into smaller garden plots.

Raised Non-dig Gardens: Good for Bad Backs

Raised garden beds are being used in centres for the handicapped and at retirement centres for the elderly throughout the world. They have become increasingly popular with elderly persons, people with back problems or for those that have some lingering injury or disability. The garden beds can be filled using any of the non-dig systems described, the basic difference being that they are well above soil level in built-up beds, boxes, troughs or containers. An elevated bed allows you to garden without having to bend and can be the same size as an ordinary garden bed or a tiny area.

Raised non-dig gardens are good for bad backs as they allow gardening without too much bending. This one is built on top of an old bed frame,

A one-bale non-dig garden planted with many companion plants including carrots, corn, cucumber, lettuce, onions, silver beet and tomatoes.

Before. This is a simple portable non-dig garden made using a bag of peat moss.

After. The same plants three weeks later with a stake in place and fruits beginning to set.

Non-dig Gardens for Children (and Gardeners Who Like It Easy)

For children and other gardeners who are not capable of much exercise, are handicapped, or who just like it easy, the following non-digs are ideal.

GROW-BAGS
You need:

a bagful of mix	a funnel
tomato seedlings	diluted liquid fertiliser

A simple grow-bag can be made using a bagful of copra peat, peat moss or soil mix. Poke holes for drainage in the bottom of the bag and slits on the top. Place the tomato plants in the slits. Watering can be done by inserting a plastic funnel into the top of the bag and pouring in the water whenever the soil mix is dry. Diluted liquid fertiliser will need to be added when you water. Add a little lime often.

HAY BALE GARDEN
You need:

one bale of hay (e.g. clover, lucerne, lupin, pasture hay or straw, peat moss)	a liquid seaweed product a supply of animal manure (pelletised or loose)
well-rotted compost or copra peat	organic fertiliser
tomato seedlings (one for a small bale, two for a large bale)	lime

1   Make a small deep hole in the bale and fill this with some compost or copra peat. Place a tomato plant deeply into this, remove some leaves and cover the stem.
2   Water the plant and soak the bale with the liquid seaweed.
3   Place pelletised or loose manure around the top of the bale, but not too close to the tomato plant stem.
4   Water with liquid seaweed whenever the compost starts to look dry. When the plant starts to grow well, apply organic fertilisers and a little lime often.

The well-aerated material will allow good growth of the tomato plant and its roots will grow out into the surrounding composting bale which will actually compost and rot down.

Some organic gardeners use several bales or huge round bales with great success.

2.2 Growing in Pots

Gardeners living in small units, flats or high-rise apartments can grow tomatoes in pots. Tomatoes are very hardy and can survive practically anything: pot-bound situations, low light, enclosed well-lit rooms and exposed positions. If you only have limited gardening space and the growing area has become diseased, placing your plants in containers, raised above the infected soil, may be the only way to grow them.

Tomatoes can be grown in compost bins, old tubs, half wine barrels, recycled polystyrene fruit boxes, cement or terracotta pipes, plastic bags, a pile of old tyres or any other type of container you can find. When growing plants in containers you need to provide good drainage.

Calendar of Things to Do

The author carried out some field experiments growing tomatoes in pots and containers with Mr Alan Kingsbury of Cheltenham, Victoria, Australia. Alan and Allen's method of growing early ripening tomatoes in cool regions can be adopted by any gardener experiencing cool to cold early spring and early summer weather conditions. In hot climates, early tomatoes can be grown at any time with the help of the protective structures described in chapter 3.4.

Winter — Plant the Seeds
Start preparations very early if you want to grow your own seedlings. The seed can be sown in early winter. See pp. 5–10 for the steps to follow.

Early Spring — Transplant into Pots
During the first week in late winter or early spring when the seedlings have grown 2 to 3 cm (1 in) tall, they can be transplanted into 1 L (¼ gallon) pots. See pp. 12–13 for the steps to follow. The seedlings should be planted deeper than they were in the previous container as this allows more roots to grow from the covered stem (see p. 14). The pots should then be placed in a sheltered position which receives plenty of sun and warmth, such as behind a recycled sheet of glass on the sunny side of a shed.

Spring — Bigger Pots
Within seven weeks of planting the seedlings into individual containers, they will have grown well enough to be transferred to 20 L (4 or 5 gallon) containers. Any type of recycled pot that is available can be used. Polystyrene fruit containers are good as they retain more heat than plastic drums and so protect the

Late winter. These seeds were planted three weeks ago. Some growth has just appeared, so they need to be squirted with liquid seaweed extract to promote good health and root growth.

Early spring. Transplant seedlings into larger pots. Both of these plants can be transferred into the 1 L (½ gallon) pot in the middle.

Spring. Roots of plants showing excellent distribution and growth within the pots. These can now be transplanted into 20 L (4-5 gallon) pots. You can see the flowers showing here. When pollinated, they will become fruits.

Late spring. Stake the plants, prune if necessary and fertilise constantly. You can see some green tomatoes.

Early summer. Alan Kingsbury, co-producer of the potted plant system, is picking his early tomatoes.

Foil has been used to protect against heat causing roots to boil in very hot weather.

plants. Fill just over half the drum or container with potting mix and plant the seedling into this. A suggested potting mix is:

- 50:50 sandy loam and compost
- a small handful of a mix of 5:1 blood and bone and sulphate of potash to promote growth and flowering
- a tablespoon of lime to prevent blossom end rot

Extra potting mix can be used to cover the stems gradually as the plants grow, but make sure that at least 20 cm (8 in) of leafy growth always remains above soil level. When fertilising, feed a little and often and back it up with liquid seaweed soil drenches to improve root growth.

Late Spring—Prune, Fertilise and Stake

During the first week of early summer the plants may be pruned to leave only one or two main shoots; this is optional.

Keep feeding the potted plants with slow-release fertiliser or pelletised organic fertiliser. Make four holes in the area around the plant's root system with a stick and put one teaspoon of fertiliser into each of the four holes.

At this time, stakes or a trellis can be installed in or near the pots to support the plants.

Early Summer—Pick the Tomatoes!

If all has gone well, gardeners in cool-climate areas will be picking their first tomatoes during early summer. At this time the plants need plenty of extra food, so apply some more slow-release fertiliser or pelletised organic fertiliser. Once the plants begin to crop, weekly or fortnightly applications of a liquid fertiliser or manure tea will assist fruit production. If the weather is extremely hot, the pots can be painted white on the outside or metal foil can be wrapped around them to reflect the heat and prevent the roots being burnt.

> ### BOILED ROOTS
> Symptoms of boiled roots are droopy leaves that don't recover with watering. The plant will stop growing. To resurrect a plant with boiled roots, prune it slightly to reduce stress. Poke holes in the potting mix and drench it with liquid seaweed. Place a small stake in the pot and cover the whole plant and pot with a sealed plastic bag. Make sure the plastic does not touch the plant leaves. Put it in a shady area for three or four days.

Midsummer—Cut Back, Protect, Mulch and Water

Tall tomato plants can be cut off at about 2 m (6 ft) from the base but if gardeners choose not to prune that's okay. Low-growing bushy plants will not need pruning. Weekly or fortnightly liquid feeds should continue and the pots will need protection from heat if that has not been given beforehand. Plants in pots may need watering at least twice a day and sometimes three times a day during very hot weather to prevent the plants becoming stressed and thus more susceptible to pest and disease attack. The use of water-absorbing granules in the soil mix will reduce the need for frequent watering and will be essential in areas where hot dry weather conditions are experienced. Placing an organic mulch around the plants will also reduce stress.

Midsummer. These have been pruned back to allow air and prevent diseases. They are being given weekly or fortnightly liquid feeds and have been protected from sun and wind. Watering is done two or three times daily.

Late Summer—Pull up

Depending on the variety of tomato, its cropping habit and the weather conditions, plants may or may not be pulled from the soil at the end of the summer period. When they start to die off they can be hung upside down in a shed so that the green tomatoes still on the plant will ripen, or the green fruit can be used to make tomato chutney.

If you have a covered, sheltered, warm area, such as a sheltered courtyard or a greenhouse, tomatoes can actually be grown continuously for several years. There are records of tomatoes growing in a heated greenhouse which have kept growing and producing for at least seven years.

Late summer. These plants have been pulled out (roots and all) and placed against a protected shed wall.

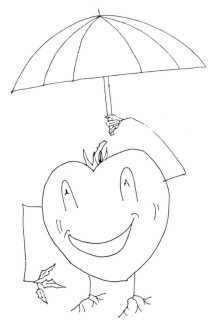

Potted Gardens for Children

Potted gardens can be made very easily. All types of containers can be used: recycled polystyrene fruit boxes, old plastic or metal drums, milk carton crates, compost bins, hats, shoes or boots, tea pots, bath tubs or socks. Use your imagination. Choose something that might otherwise be thrown away, such as an old washing tub, and help prevent pollution of the environment.

HANGING BASKET MADE FROM AN OLD HAT

1　Buy, scrounge, borrow or collect a discarded floppy tennis hat from someone. The hat can be painted or dyed if you want it to be colourful.
2　Tie strong cord to three sides of the hat by scrunching up three parts of the brim and tying the cord around it. Pull the three pieces together to make a pyramid above the hat and tie them so that the hat hangs evenly when the cord is held.
3　Fill the hat with compost that has a pinch of lime and some water-absorbent granules added to it.
4　Plant one or several tomato plants in the hat (cherry tomatoes are best).
5　Water the plants with liquid seaweed and place a few pellets of pelletised organic fertiliser on top of the compost (but not against the tomato plant stems).
6　Now you have a hanging basket! Hang it in a position that receives sunlight for most of the day but is protected from the late afternoon sun.
7　Water and feed regularly.

2.3 Using Hydroponics

One of the easiest and most convenient methods of growing tomatoes is by hydroponics. Hydroponic gardening entails growing plants in a non-organic material instead of soil and using flowing or partially flowing liquid nutrient solutions to feed them. The non-organic material which is called the medium is used merely to support the plants, hold the nutrient solution, and provide drainage and protection. It doesn't itself contain nutrients. However, unlike soil, it doesn't contain weed seeds or diseases either. Mediums used in hydroponics include washed river sand, scoria, sand, gravel, perlite or vermiculite. The plants are fed with a liquid that contains dissolved nutrients of most of the elements needed for a plant's growth. Hydroponic plants usually look much healthier than conventional grown ones, because there is little opportunity for pests and diseases to invade them.

Hydroponic tomatoes, like container-grown tomatoes can be grown almost anywhere:

in small gardens
in pots or bags
on walls
in protected greenhouses

on sunny veranda areas
inside enclosed rooms (using special plant lights to supply light)

But Is It Organic?

Organic gardening purists will say that, because the plants are not in contact with the soil, the system cannot be classified as organic. However, although no one has yet perfected a useable completely organic nutrient solution, gardeners can prepare their own liquids from organic materials and manures if they wish to grow organically. Guano, a liquid fertiliser prepared from bat poo, is one organic medium used for hydroponic growing.

Systems

There are many hydroponic systems and different sized modules are available to suit large commercial growers, keen gardeners or one-plant hobbyists. They vary in the methods used to supply the nutrient, the frequency of its application and the kind of medium, if any, that is used. Using some of the modern gardening materials available, gardeners can improvise and easily make their very own hyroponic gardening kit.

A commercial hydroponic system where the plants are grown in scoria beds under an igloo.

The Simplest System: Self-watering Pot

The simplest example of a hydroponic system is a self-watering pot. This is a pot with a reservoir at the bottom holding a nutrient solution which is drawn up into the pot by capillary action, so that feeding and watering occurs slowly over a long period of time. The nutrient solution only needs to be added when the reservoir indicator shows the level as critical. See also p. 38 for instructions on how to make your own self-watering pot.

Wick System

A reservoir of nutrient solution is placed at the same level near, under, or slightly above the plant and a rough wick of frayed rope, cotton or other absorbent material is placed with one end of the wick in the water and the other in the medium or near the plant roots. Nutrient solution is slowly drawn by capillary action along the wick to the tomato plants. A simple wick system consists of nutrient-filled wine flagons and accompanying wick for every tomato plant in the garden bed. The flagons should be refilled every few days whenever they become near dry.

Recycling System

With most hydroponic systems the released nutrient solution is collected or pumped into a header tank (holding tank) and continuously recycled. These systems can be fully automatic. Continuous irrigation of plants with the nutrient mix is provided on a stop–start cycle where nutrients are flooded through the systems or pots for a short period of time then allowed to drain out for several hours before the next wave of irrigation is given. The nutrient solutions have to be completely replaced every 10 to 14 days if damage to plants and burning of the root systems is to be avoided. This is because the liquid evaporates, especially in hot weather, causing a build-up of acidity, alkalinity or just an oversupply of one or two of the nutrients in the mix because others fall out as salts.

A homemade hydroponics system on very well drained soil, where nutrients are not recycled but allowed to trickle continuously into the raised garden beds.

MAKE YOUR OWN

You can easily make a hydroponic recycling system from bits and pieces:

a recycled enclosed container to use as a header tank 10 to 20 L (2 to 5 gal)	microtubing to feed nutrients to individual plants pots
an on−off tap	black plastic sheeting
some plastic tubing to use as nutrient flow tubes	a bucket or suitable container a small water pump

1 Set up the header tank (recycled container) above the level of the plants to be watered so that you can feed them using gravity.
2 Insert/attach the on−off tap to the container and connect tubing from it to the rows of plants.
3 From this, smaller tubing can be fed out to the individual plants, pots or garden beds.
4 Set up a slightly sloped surface on which to place the pots and cover this with black plastic. The pots that the plants are growing in will drain onto the plastic sheeting and, because it is slightly sloped, the nutrient then flows down into a plastic bucket.
5 Set up a small pump to lift the drained-off nutrients from the plastic bucket back to the header tank so they can be recycled.

Usually the nutrient flow tap is turned on long enough to flood-irrigate all the plants being watered. Irrigation times vary, but may be as little as twice a day depending on the system and substrate used to anchor the plants.

Some hydroponic systems use an absorbent matting placed on a gently sloping bench. Nutrient solution is continuously flowing along the matting. The solution soaks up from the matting into the medium in the pot and then to the plant's roots.

Pots on Nutrient Mats

One of the newest ideas in hydroponics is to put the tomato plants partially into an enclosed hollow container with the roots of the plants hanging free into space. The plants are secured within holes with pegs or plugs of soft material. A very fine mist of the nutrient solution is misted continuously onto the root system inside the container. Root growth is extremely vigorous and the plants perform well.

No Medium, Just Space

A simple hydroponic system has been tried by Dr Struan Sutherland, author of *Hydroponics for Everyone*. A polystyrene sheet (or chunk of recycled polystyrene material) with a punched in hole to hold the plant is floated in a 5 L (2 gal) bucket filled with nutrient solution. The roots of the plant grow through the polystyrene into the solution and the plant is grown virtually on a floating island.

A Polystyrene Island

SELF-WATERING POT FOR CHILDREN

You need:

a small pot	a cherry tomato plant
soil mix	water
a plastic coke bottle	a seaweed product
750 mL (1½ pints)	

1 Use a small pot with drainage holes.

2 Fill the pot with a good soil mix, copra peat, palm peat or peat moss. Pelletised slow-release organic fertilisers can be placed on the surface of the soil mix in the pot.

3 Place or squeeze the pot inside another see-through non-draining pot or container (e.g. half a coke bottle) leaving an air gap between the base of the inside pot and the base of the see-through container.

4 Plant a tomato plant (try one of the small cherry tomato varieties) in the small pot and water with a seaweed product.

5 Add water, allowing it to just touch the base of the small inside pot.

6 A string wick can be threaded out of the drainage holes of the small pot into the water but this is not essential.

7 Keep checking the see-through container and fill with water every time the water level falls below the base of the small pot.

8 Spray the leaves of the tomato plant for extra nutrients if the leaves start to look yellow. Only wet the leaves at the beginning of the day, so as to allow the leaf surface time to dry before nightfall.

2.4 Companion and Mixed-species Planting

One way to make sure that tomato plants remain healthy, happy and virtually free of pests and diseases is to include companion plants in the tomato patch or near pots containing tomato plants. Companion plants are those which, when planted with tomatoes, produce a beneficial effect. Companion planting and mixed-species planting (planting a whole lot of different types of plants in the one garden area) used in combination with mulching, organic gardening principles and the non-use of chemicals will benefit tomato plants and help reduce the number of pests and outbreaks of disease within the tomato patch. Permaculture gardeners use guilds. These are small garden areas containing many mixed types of plants and there are many guilds within the designed garden.

Tomato and Basil Basil is one companion plant to tomatoes that has been proved beneficial in research by the late Hank Swaan and students at the Victorian College of Agriculture and Horticulture. They recommend planting four basil plants around each tomato plant for the best results. Tests

Tomatoes respond very well when planted next to basil. Basil usually requires higher temperatures, though, so use a plastic bottle or a mini-greenhouse to provide extra warmth around the plant.

showed that tomatoes grown with basil plants actually cropped better and that basil grown with tomatoes grew into large productive plants, thus each plant acted as a companion plant to the other. The reason that basil is beneficial to tomato plants and vice versa probably has something to do with the following:

- basil plant roots opening up the soil around the tomato plants providing extra oxygen to the soil
- the cooling effect of partial shading of basil plants and soil surface (which also reduces weed seedling growth)
- the repellent nature of the aromatic scent given off by the basil leaves deterring insects and pests

The actual effect of one individual companion plant on another varies. A few of the helpful qualities demonstrated by companion plants are described below.

Other Companion Plants

Shading

CLIMBERS SHADE TOMATOES
Chinese tomato growers plant their tomato seedlings in trenches, then grow climbing beans or other climbing plants on a teepee structure over the seedlings to give them protection, save space, increase cropping and conserve water.

TOMATOES SHADE SMALLER PLANTS
Tall-growing tomato plants that need staking can be staked within a teepee shape, leaving a triangular space under the structure for other plants. Plants such as beans, celery, endive, lettuce or radish can be planted under the teepee and be protected by the growing tomato plants. This type of arrangement is a way of companion planting and allows for bountiful food production. An irrigation trench can be dug in the sheltered area to prevent excessive water loss through evaporation.

Daisy-type multi-petalled flowers provide a great source of pollen to help predators overwinter during cold periods. Here a native Australian wasp feeds on the nectar of a mature daisy flower.

Providing or Recycling Nutrients

- Generally speaking, legume plants such as clover and peas can be used to provide the nutrient nitrogen to the soil. See Green Manure (p. 49) or Mulches (chapter 3.2).
- Dandelion and some other deep-rooted plants can mine the lower soil depths and bring leached nutrients back to the surface. When the dandelions die down or are mulch mowed, the rotting mulch provides these nutrients to the other plants or soil organisms and encourages worms which fertilise the soil.

Attracting Predator Insects and Spiders

- *Phacelia*, the forget-me-not (*Myosotis* species) and the common shasta daisy (*Leucanthemum* × *superbum*) all attract and provide food pollen for hover flies. Hover fly larvae are voracious feeders, consuming thousands of aphids, and are essential in the garden to provide some measure of biological insect control.
- Daisy-type plants, such as the Easter daisy (*Aster novi-belgii*), and plants in the Umbelliferae family, for example lovage, carrots or parsnips (allowed to flower), can be used to supply pollen for predatory wasps which in turn feed on insects and grubs.
- Mixed-species plantings will attract other predators, such as praying mantids, hover flies, ladybirds, lacewings and spiders.

Attracting Pollinating Insects

- Lavender attracts bees and other insects that initiate pollination.

Attracting Birds

- Try growing some local indigenous plants and nectar-producing plants; these will attract birds and insect predators. Even the lowly household sparrow can be seen inspecting tomato plants and collecting insects from them for food.
- Bottlebrush and other Australian plants attract many birds that help keep insects under control.

☙ Garlic root exudates contain sulphur compounds that may inhibit the growth of harmful fungi and bacteria.

Inhibiting Fungi and Bacteria

Aromatic plants give off perfume or scents that can prevent pest insects from finding their target plant.

Distracting or Repelling Insects

☙ Basil is an insect repellent.
☙ Nasturtiums will attract aphids away from tomato plants.
☙ Marigolds and pyrethrum are reported to repel thrips.
☙ Some species of marigold supposedly repel eelworms.
☙ Wormwood helps repel insects.

☙ Carnivorous plants, such as the venus fly trap, can actually trap and digest insects.

Trapping Insects

☙ Flowering tobacco plants (*Nicotiana* species) have sticky leaves that trap flying insects. These plants are not the ones that are used to make tobacco.

One example of companion planting with tomatoes was done by Mr Ken Hawkey. He group-planted alyssum, verbena, carnations, pelargoniums, bonfire salvia, and *Epacris colorins* 'White Delight' and allowed a self-sown tomato plant to grow among them (this plant came from the compost placed around the plants). The surrounding plants attracted lots of bees, butterflies and many nectar birds were attracted to the epacris. The effect of the birds (eating insects as well as nectar), the protection of the nearby plants, the partial shading by companion plants and the biologically active organic soil, all provided excellent growth conditions for the tomato plant. This method produced huge crops of tomatoes.

Mixed-species Planting

Ken Hawkey's tomato bush surrounded by companion plants.

Companion Planting for Children

TOMATO AND BASIL

When children plant their tomato plants, they can place a basil plant with them:

1 Place manure pellets and lime on the garden bed and dig in.
2 Make a hole for your tomato seedling and put it in the hole.
3 Cover the soil over the roots and water with a liquid seaweed product.
4 Plant a basil seedling beside the tomato seedling but cover it with half a plastic bottle to keep it warm.

TOMATOES AND FLOWERS

Flower seeds such as daisies can be sown around the base of the tomato plant after it has been planted in the garden. Lightly cover the seeds with compost or soil and water well.

A non-dig garden planted with tomatoes and basil. Children can place open-ended plastic drink bottles over the basil plants to ensure the growth rates of the tomato and basil remain equal.

Potted tomatoes grown by Jack Simpson in his backyard—a beefsteak selection he called 'Russian Red'.

3 General Care

Well-staked tomato plants. The straw mulch suppresses weed growth, keeps the roots moistened during summer, builds up biological activity in the soil and prevents water run-off.

3.1 Feeding

For good growth, tomato plants need a regular supply of the basic food elements, nitrogen, potassium and phosphorus, as well as a sufficient quantity of calcium, sulphur, magnesium, manganese, zinc, copper and many other micro-nutrients. Micro-nutrients are usually required in very small amounts (of parts per million or parts per billion) so a little goes a long, long way. These elements can be supplied by well-prepared compost that has had lots of different organic materials, manure and scraps added to it during the composting process. **Nutrients for Tomatoes**

Before the development of chemical fertilisers in the early 1900s, all farm produce and home-grown vegetables were produced by organic methods. Gardeners who want to look after the environment and grow food without using chemicals are returning to these methods. **Chemical Fertilisers**

Chemical fertilisers are made from base materials, usually changed chemically by acids or alkalis into a product that can easily be taken up by plant roots. Most chemical fertilisers are very soluble in water and it is with water that plants 'ingest' their food in the form of the three main plant foods nitrogen, phosphorus, potassium and the many other minor elements. Fertilisers are available in various forms including pellets, coated granules, powders, crystals and liquids for foliar application. Because they are easily absorbed, in most cases they will produce spectacular lush green plants full of vigour and soft growth, which is often exactly what a farmer or gardener wants to see.

The down side of chemical fertilisers is that the plants become more susceptible to pests and diseases, they require constant applications because the fertilisers are very soluble in water and wash away from the root zone, and the edible plant tissue often contains unhealthy amounts of some elements such as nitrogen.

Moreover, the water containing the dissolved chemical fertilisers seeps down into the watertable in the soil and feeds into rivers and streams. Then the polluted water in rivers and streams runs into the oceans causing massive pollution and disruption of the life forms wherever it goes. Run-off pollution is a major contribution to the degradation of our river systems and oceans. Although organic fertilisers can also cause run-off pollution, it only occurs when they are overused.

The main difference between chemical fertilisers and organic fertilisers is that *all* organisms within the soil benefit from organic fertilisers, directly and indirectly. Some organic fertilisers, like manure, when deposited on the soil, already contain bacteria and fungi and microscopic animal populations. *All* organic fertilisers, when they are exposed to an open-air environment, attract tiny animals, bacteria and fungi, then worms. Many of these organisms and animals produce organic acids which create nutrient-rich humus, the backbone of organic gardening. Humus absorbs many times its weight of water and slowly releases nutrients over a long period of time. In soils containing humus, the nutrients are not entirely lost by leaching and are available to growing **Organic Fertilisers**

plants. Chemical fertilisers often kill off the organisms that are responsible for producing humus.

Many gardeners, and some garden writers, call compost 'humus',
which is incorrect. Humus is a by-product of biological activity (e.g. the
composting process); mature compost will contain some humus material.

Scientists have found that most living plants have bacteria or fungi
living near their roots or have organisms growing within their tissue
which act to transfer nutrients. This association of separate life forms
which help each other is called symbiosis. A simple example of symbiosis
is the rhizobium bacteria of legumes (plants in the pea family). This
bacteria lives on their roots, producing cell-like structures containing
nitrogen. When the plant dies the nitrogen is available to nearby plants.
High concentrations of chemical fertilisers kill these useful bacteria and
fungi.

There are many types of organic materials used by gardeners to feed
tomato plants and to build up soils. Some of them are listed below.

Compost

Compost is recommended as the main ingredient to supply nutrients to
tomatoes (see chapter 3.2).

Manures

Manure from any animal, if it is available, can be used in the organic
garden. Popular manures are chicken, cow, sheep, horse, pigeon, goat
and pig. Some special manures, like elephant, emu and ostrich, can
sometimes be found. Tomatoes thrive when fed this kind of natural
organic food.

Fresh Manure

Fresh manures are very high in nutrient content and must be used very
sparingly and a few weeks before planting time. Place fresh manure well
below the plant root systems or incorporate it with other mulching
material such as grass clippings, sawdust, shredded newspaper or autumn
leaves, because if it is near the plant roots it will burn them.

Most organic gardeners use manure after it has had time to self-
compost or they dig it into the soil well before planting time. They may
also incorporate manure into compost heaps or piles then use the
composted material when it has matured. See p. 70 for information of
the problem with polluted manure.

Zoo Poo

Innovative persons at zoos and animal parks have started packaging
'Zoo Poo'. This product from animals at zoos is available to home
gardeners in limited supplies.

Pelletised Manure

Pelletised manure is a slow-release fertiliser, gradually releasing nutrients
into the surrounding soil. The manure is compressed so it is reduced in
volume, very portable and convenient to use. It is one-fifth the volume
of fresh manure. Large compressed pellets intended for trees are also
available and these have been used successfully around tomato plants.

Manure Teas

Many gardeners prepare an organic liquid fertiliser, often called a 'tea',
from manure by soaking it in drums. A shovelful of manure is placed in

a drum of water and left to soak for a few days. The liquid is then poured off and used as a root drench or as a foliar spray on the leaves of plants. Some gardeners find it easier to suspend the manure in an open mesh bag within the drum of water. The tea is diluted with about ten parts of water for foliar and soil applications. Some gardeners use cow manure tea to feed their tomatoes every day during the growing season.

Other Teas

Another liquid tea used with great success on tomatoes is stinging nettle tea which can be prepared by soaking the fresh or dried leaves in water (see p. 14). The leaves must be fermented before use. Tea can be prepared from other ingredients such as herbs and compost.

Worm Castings (Vermicast)

Worm castings from a gardener's own worm farm or compost heap will provide some nutrients to plants. Castings are excreted by worms as they digest their own weight in soil and organic material every day. During the passage of this material through the worm, it is concentrated and forms a moist crumbly end-product. Worm castings have many times more nutrients in them than the surrounding soil from which they were made, and this is why they are a perfect organic fertiliser. Dead worms also supply nutrients to the soil.

Worm farm kits are available to home gardeners and any gardener can turn a compost heap or compost bin into a worm farm if they want to (see p. 55). Biologically active soil contains many worms.

Worm castings used by themselves in open gardens may become slightly waterlogged in wet conditions, so the addition of composted or shredded dry materials to open up the mixture and provide extra aeration will be beneficial. Castings can be spread as a 5 to 10 cm (2 to 4 in) layer on top of non-dig garden beds. Worm castings mixed with other good draining material, such as newspaper or washed sand, have been used for potting and propagation mixes for tomato seedlings.

Fish Products

Millions of fish are caught and killed every day for human consumption, for the making of pet food and for other products. About two-thirds of the fish, including the skin, scales, bones, head and stomach, is disposed of. As well as being wasteful, the ways it is disposed of are also very damaging to the environment. Scientists have started to recycle it into food for plants.

Fish products are ideal for plants because they stimulate the soil. They are available in two forms: either as a concentrated emulsion or composted and mixed with organic matter. The liquid emulsions are useful for drenching the soil and for foliar sprays. The composted fish products are useful as mulches.

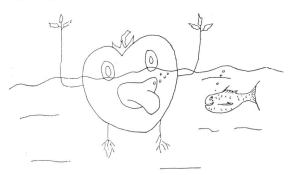

Seaweed Products

Seaweed has been used as a fertiliser for hundreds of years by farmers living near good supplies. In some places, composted seaweed has been the only material used to grow crops. Any seaweed can be composted and used in the garden provided that its collection is permitted by local and environmental authorities, so before you collect from the beach, ring your local council. Harvesting of living seaweed from the ocean is not recommended because of the disruption it causes to marine animal habitats.

Seaweed absorbs all its nutrients from the rich nutritional soup of the ocean. Although they are in small quantities, almost all the known elements occur in seaweed, including gold! Large flat-leafed kelps and the chain-bubble type of seaweeds have the most nutrients. At the other extreme, seagrass has hardly any nutrient value, although it is useful as a mulch, or as an addition to the compost heap. All kinds of seaweed contain lots of micro-nutrients and scientists have found that they also have hormone-like materials that stimulate the growth of plant roots.

Commercial seaweed products are available as a powder or as a liquid. They can be used in composts and mulches, as foliar and soil drenches, and to spray the leaves and fruit to improve pest and disease resistance.

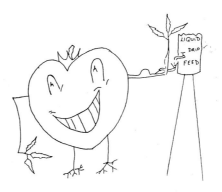

Toilet Waste

The popular septic tank is one of the worst sewage systems ever developed and the direct disposal of human waste into the oceans from cities is one of the disasters of our time. It pollutes the ocean instead of providing much-needed life to our soils. We need to rethink the way our waste material is disposed of, and composting toilets or fully enclosed toilet processing facilities may provide an alternative by recycling it back into the soil. Different kinds of composting toilets are already available and some councils allow their use. Other councils and some health authorities forbid the use of material derived from human waste for growing food plants for human consumption, or require the material to be buried in the soil well away from contact with plants and their root systems.

Compost from composting toilets provides nutrients and humus to the soil.

This product is a huge resource available in some nurseries but is not yet common. It is the partially decomposed material that has not yet formed into black coal. It is a fine, fibrous and crumbly material that can be used in an organic garden to supply nutrients and help build up the humus content in the soil. It should be used sparingly, though, as a 10 per cent component of soil mixes or dusted over the tomato patch at a rate of about one handful per square metre (square yard).

Brown Coal

Humic acid, a gel-like substance produced from biological activity in the soil, is available in liquid form for foliar application or as a soil drench. It is not needed on small organic gardens where the biological activity is already high. A rich compost usually supplies all the humates needed. But if your soil is poor or sandy, humic acid can bring life to it. Humic acid benefits the soil in the same way as humus (see p. 45–6). It also improves cropping, stimulates seed germination, encourages fibrous root production of plants and provides some minor nutrients. It can be used in pots.

Humic Acid

Green manure refers to plants grown specifically so they can be harvested and dug back into the soil before they are fully mature. Plants commonly grown as green manure are legumes such as lupins, clovers, lucerne and peas—cowpeas and dolichos beans in warm-climate areas—and cereals (wheat, buckwheat and oats). The plants to be used are broadcast-sown so they grow thick and bushy and when they are almost mature (usually at about the time when they flower), they are dug straight back into the ground. Green manure crops benefit the soil in the same way as mulches and composts (see p. 51). They also control weeds and can be used to give the soil a break from other plants. Wheat and oats grown as rotation crops can control eelworms, tiny worm-like creatures which cause lumpy growths to appear on tomato plant roots.

Green Manure

Research has shown that plants are healthier and produce more when mineral fertilisers are used in combination with organic fertilisers and organic matter. Mineral and rock dust products are powders available from some fertiliser companies. Examples are:

Specific Nutrients

Mineral and Rock Dust Products

- ✿ ground rock **phosphate** (P)
- ✿ ground rock **sulphur** (S)
- ✿ ground rock limestone to provide **calcium** (Ca)

Rocks, such as granite and basalt, contain lots of the minerals and nutrients necessary for plant growth. The dust needs to be dug into the garden several months before planting because it takes time for the nutrients to be biologically released from the dust particles. All the major nutrients can be obtained from raw rock without the rock having to be chemically treated and some of the cement-producing rock-crushing plants working in highly mineralised rock sites can provide low-cost rock dust for home gardeners. They should be used very sparingly as a light application of dust because the materials are very stable. When storing the material, make sure it is in a very dry place where it will not get wet and set like concrete.

Blood and Bone

There are many brands of blood and bone available on the market. However, some have very little actual blood and bone in them and instead have other fertilisers added or lots of compost material to 'bulk them up'. As a rule of thumb, the more expensive the product the more blood and bone it will contain!

Blood and bone has a relatively high **nitrogen** content, contains some phosphorus but no potassium, and very few of the trace elements. However, it releases its nitrogen very quickly and may burn plants if too much is used. Many gardeners mix blood and bone with a mulch material such as sawdust to prevent it from burning their plants.

Hoof and Horn

Hoof and horn is similar in nutrient content to blood and bone (it also has lots of **nitrogen**). However, it releases the nutrients much more slowly, so is used as a slow-release fertiliser.

Urea

Urea comes from urine. Fresh urine is used by many organic gardeners and is widely used in China where farmers have been practising organic gardening and farming for centuries. It was not long ago that all Australian households had a lemon tree at the back door that received regular applications of fresh urine.

Urine smells strongly and is very high in **nitrogen** so it needs to be fermented for a while or diluted before use. The usual rate of dilution is 10:1. This solution can be applied to tomato leaves without burning the foliage or it can be watered into and around the root zone of the plants several times a week. Urine can also be used as a direct nitrogen supply to the compost heap.

Urea can be chemically manufactured into slow-release forms that are very safe to use. Organic gardeners do not advocate the use of manufactured urea, but they may eventually accept it because, structurally, it does not differ from the natural product.

Wood Ash

> Wood ash is a fine talc-like powder usually collected from open fire sites. It contains a lot of **potash (potassium)** but this is locked up and unavailable to the plants unless organic acids, which can be provided by compost, are present in the soil or potting mix. So, if you use lots of wood ash, you must also use plenty of compost. This is especially important in heavy soils because the fine particles can plug up the pores, reducing aeration and making the soil gluggy. Compost will free the soil up. Some gardeners add wood ash to the compost mix heap and then spread the mature compost around their plants. It can be used liberally on sandy or well-drained shale soils. It is extremely alkaline so must not be used on alkaline soils or too close to plants.

3.2 Composts and Mulches

Composts and mulches:
- build up the biological activity within the soil and create humus (see p. 45–6)
- cool the roots of tomato plants during hot weather and prevent the topsoil being washed away by the hose or sudden thunderstorms
- retain water and prevent drying out
- act as a weed control barrier when spread 10 cm (4 in) deep
- allow tomato plants to form extra roots in well-aerated material
- warm plant roots during cool weather (due to the heat given off by the composting process)

Composts

During the composting process, materials are broken down by organisms and micro-organisms into nutrients that are easily absorbed by the roots of plants. Tomatoes grow well in humus-rich soils so thrive when grown in organic material. They always seem to do well as 'volunteer' plants when they have self-germinated in compost heaps. Some gardeners actually 'seed' their compost with a squashed tomato fruit so that they are almost guaranteed tomato seedlings each season. They argue that any seed germinated naturally grows at the correct time of year and is more likely to survive and be resistant to cool weather and pests and diseases.

Practitioners of biodynamics, permaculture, self-sufficiency and organic gardening use compost as the major supplier of nutrients for tomato plants. Compost is easy to prepare and there are many different ways of making it.

Most composted materials have very low amounts of the main nutrients nitrogen, potassium and phosphate, but they do contain tiny amounts of many micro-nutrients (nutrients used by tomato plants in very small quantities) and they are very good for the soil. To obtain the greatest benefit to the soil or potting mix, the composted material should be used as quickly as possible after preparation.

Composting Methods

There are many different ways of composting and the period needed for the compost to mature can vary from as little as a few weeks to several months or even one whole year or more depending on the method used. Slow composting occurs when there is not much heat or air and where the heap is not often turned. Faster heaps are those that get very hot. These are good for killing any pathogens and weed seeds. Worms are active in most compost heaps, but gardeners using the hot composting system will not see any worms in their bins.

The key to compost success is the carbon–nitrogen ratio of the materials used. Paper, for instance, is just carbon and will not compost unless a form or nitrogen, such as animal manure or lawn clippings, is added to it. Lawn clippings, on the other hand, will compost without the addition of other materials as their carbon–nitrogen ratio is ideal. It is usually agreed that the carbon–nitrogen ratio should be about 30:1, but gardeners can use their own judgement when preparing compost.

Providing the materials compost well there is no need to be too specific about the ratios.

People usually just throw all their waste materials into the compost bin on a daily basis and eventually the bin may fill up with compost. Some bins are very efficient at reducing bulk and worms help by operating at the base of the bin and spreading the compost into the surrounding soil. It looks as if the bin never fills up and rarely has any ready-to-use compost in it, but the soil under the bin will be black and rich with compost nutrients and organic matter.

Gardeners with a more scientific approach *fill their bins* with layers of chosen materials (any organic material can be used) to increase efficiency and obtain a good carbon−nitrogen ratio of materials. Some tips for layering are:

- Cut-up pruning twigs supply aeration and are usually placed at the base of the bin.
- It helps if water is sprinkled on each layer as the materials are applied. An ideal moisture content is reached when a handful of compost material is squeezed and will release only three or four drops of water.
- Dry shredded paper or sawdust will soak up any excess moisture and should be used on top of wet materials such as green grass or vegetable matter.
- A sprinkle of lime reduces acidity (in open composts) and provides calcium.
- Animal manure or grass clippings supply nitrogen.

Layering and filling the bin speeds up the composting process.

Right: A half bin showing how to provide extra aeration with plastic piping and how to fill the compost bin completely using as many types of material as possible, including animal manure, herbs, zeolite, and liquid seaweed.

Extreme right: The almost-completed layered compost with aeration pipes inserted. Note that the layer of paper towelling has still to rot down. Some materials take a long time to compost properly and this is why it is best to mix the materials together (see above) rather than layer them.

This method makes the composting material very hot for several days so that weed seeds, pests and diseases will be killed. To create the heat required you will need to:

- ✿ fill the bin very quickly (one day is ideal)
- ✿ cover the compost heap or bin with black plastic for the first three days to retain heat and moisture and give the composting process a good start
- ✿ use a good mixture of materials
- ✿ have the compost moist but not wet (if it is too wet it will go putrid)
- ✿ omit the soil and lime applications (these slow down the composting process)
- ✿ shred *all* the material placed into the bin (this greatly speeds up the composting process)
- ✿ mix all the materials together instead of layering them so they compost quickly
- ✿ provide aeration pipes or turn the heap frequently so that all parts of the heap get equal heat
- ✿ add powdered zeolite (if available) to the compost mix to get rid of smells; some of the nutrients stored in the zeolite will act like a slow-release fertiliser

The temperature of the composting heap may reach 100°C (212°F) or more during the composting process. Temperatures of 60°C + (140°F +) for thirty minutes will pasteurise the compost, killing most weed seeds, pests and diseases. Worms will not work in temperatures above 27°C (80°F) and rats or mice will be repelled by this heat. By hot composting, mature compost can be produced in as little as *nine* days! More information on this system is in the author's book entitled *No Garbage; Composting and Recycling*.

Any type of compost bin can be used to hot compost, except worm bins.

Gardeners using this system have three or more large permanent bins placed side by side. Each bin should be able to hold at least one cubic metre (or one cubic yard) of compost material at any given time. This is the *least* amount of material necessary to start this composting process. To start an open three-bin system:

1 Fill bin 1 completely.
2 When bin 1 is full begin filling bin 2.
3 When bin 2 is partially filled, take the top layers of bin 1 and spread it over bin 2.
4 Use the mature compost left in bin 1. This will leave it empty. Keep adding to bin 2.
5 When bin 2 is full start filling bin 3.
6 When bin 3 is partially full, take the top layers of bin 2 and spread it over bin 3.
7 Use the mature compost left in bin 2 and keeping adding to bin 3.
8 When bin 3 is full, start filling bin 1 again.

It is necessary to use three bins and/or move the material from one to the other because material in the outer layers and on top of open bins does not compost properly. Because the compost is open to the air it just dries out quickly without rotting. Moving material from the top of one bin to the middle of the next allows it to decompose properly because the middle of the heap is where all the action is happening. Some gardeners with access to plenty of organic matter for composting have up to nine open bins in a row.

The usual time needed for material in open bin systems to mature is 10 to 18 months. To speed up the process dramatically and create heat (which kills pathogens) try hot composting.

Portable Bins

Portable bins are very suitable for small gardens and households that don't have large amounts of waste. They are becoming more and more popular as suburban and inner city households start to compost their organic waste rather than throw it out. They don't take up as much room as open bins and the material is kept compact and hidden. The compost bin lid is fixed on to prevent rain from making the compost too wet; it also cuts down on smells and flies.

A typical open three-bin system where material is turned from one bin to the next until all the material has composted.

A portable bin showing the amount of completed compost obtained from one full bin. This bin was filled in one operation to obtain faster results. Portable compost bins are ideal for most home gardeners, especially those living in small units or who have tiny garden areas.

Gardeners are faced with a real dilemma when trying to choose a portable bin for composting. There are so many available, and they vary in cost substantially. Many councils are now giving them away or allowing subsidies on bins purchased from city offices. In general, there is no perfect portable bin on the market; all available bins will work to some degree of efficiency but may need modifications to produce compost quickly all the year round. Usually the modifications needed are to supply extra aeration and to keep the bins warm in winter or cool in summer.

Recycled Rubbish-Bin

Gardeners with little or no money can convert a plastic rubbish bin into a compost bin. Obtain a plastic rubbish bin and cut the bottom away with a sharp knife so that you have two open ends. The bin can be used the right way up with the lid clasped in place or turned upside down with the lid resting on what was the base. Put a brick on the lid so that it won't blow away. These bins can be buried in the soil so that the top is the only part showing or placed on soil or concrete covered areas. In-ground bins can be used only where the soil is well drained. Any system of composting can be used in these bins.

COMPOSTING DOG AND CAT POO

> Tiny in-ground rubbish bins can be used as dog or cat composting loos. Just put the animal faeces in the bin, add some shredded paper or sawdust to soak up the excess moisture and a sprinkle of lime (or zeolite) to reduce odours. Some commercial models are also available to home gardeners.

Rotating Bins

A do-it-yourself rotating bin.

Most rotating bins are very expensive, but they do provide the best method of composting of all the bins available on the market. The main reason for this is that the compost in the bins can easily be turned, which speeds up the composting process. By turning them three to five times a day as recommended, extra aeration is provided and the compost matures quickly. These bins are also very portable and can be placed anywhere in the garden area. They are so clean gardeners could have one inside the house if they wanted to. For self-sufficient gardeners, rotating drum compost bins can very easily be made from recycled 200 L (44 gal) metal or plastic drums.

Worm Bins

Composting with worms is very popular, especially with those gardeners who live in flats and do not have a large amount of material to compost each day. However, as worms are killed in hot composts and weeds and diseased material will survive in the temperatures worms enjoy, you should avoid putting anything into your worm bin that you don't want in you garden! Special-purpose worm bins can be bought and most portable compost bins or open bins can be transformed into miniature worm farms just by adding worms and providing extra aeration.

Having a worm farm is a responsibility, though. It is easy to allow the bin to get too hot or too cold, feed too much high-protein food to the worms, deprive them of air, or poison them with pollutants, so make sure you follow the instructions supplied with the bins and buy a good book about worm farming (see bibliography).

Mulches

Composted material can be used as mulch in a layer on the soil around tomato plants, but there are many other materials that gardeners use for mulching.

Plastic or synthetic mulches are sometimes placed in narrow strips along tomato beds just to prevent weed growth; they inhibit weeds in different ways. However, excessive heat can build up under plastic mulch, or within waterlogged mulches and can stew or kill fine root hairs. This prevents the plants taking up food and dead roots also offer an entry point for diseases and root rot organisms (see chapter 4).

Some of the materials available for use as mulch are as follows:

- animal manures
- bagasse (sugarcane waste)
- bark chips
- copra peat or palm peat (recycled coconut fibre)
- cubed or compressed mulches, available from nurseries
- eucalyptus leaves
- Ezi Mulch pellets
- grape marc, available from vineyards/wineries
- grass clippings
- gravel
- Gro & Mulch cubes
- hair clippings
- lucerne
- mushroom compost
- paper
- pea straw
- peanut shells
- rice hulls
- sawdust
- seaweed
- wood pulp
- woodshavings
- worm castings

- aerated plastic sheeting
- black plastic sheeting
- brown plastic sheeting
- carpet underlay
- clear plastic sheeting—cooks weeds with the heat generated
- plastic chips/pieces
- silver-sided plastic sheeting—distracts flying insects
- white-sided plastic sheeting

Above: A tomato plant in compost in a recycled portable plastic carton, mulched with recycled shredded office paper. This type of mulch is low in nutrients and may need some animal manure or blood and bone sprinkled on it to help it break down. *Right top:* Shredded organic mulch material composed of bean shoots, straw, and oak leaves. *Right bottom:* Grow & Mulch cubes.

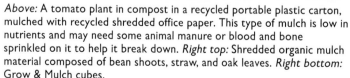

3.3 Watering

Water is becoming scarce in most parts of the world. As populations increase, so does the demand for water. One consequence is that home gardeners will have to find ways of using less water to keep costs down.

The cardinal rule of many tomato growers is '**do not water overhead**'. This may seem strange when you consider that in a natural environment tomatoes only receive water as rain from overhead, but it minimises the chances of them catching diseases. Diseases such as early or late blight and bacterial tomato speck are more likely to infect the plant if water is splashed on the leaves, spreading the disease spores. If the foliage is kept dry at night, there is less chance of this. If watering overhead, water early in the day so that leaves have time to dry.

Watering Systems

Hand-held Hose

This is probably the most common type of watering system. Unfortunately, most gardeners turn on the hose with too much force and inadvertently wash all the soil away from the top root zone of the plants. The exposed fibrous roots then become sunburned or heat stressed. It is better to use a low gentle water pressure. A heavy layer of mulch around the roots of the plants will help to dissipate the force of the water (see chapter 3.2). One advantage of hand-held hoses is that the water can be placed where it is needed and not wasted. It is a good system, provided enough time is allowed for the water to soak into the soil and high water pressure is not used.

Perforated Hoses

Rubber hoses with thin porous walls allow water to bleed gently and slowly out to the plant roots, providing an even distribution of water. A hose attached to a tap is fixed to the open end to provide the water flow. These hoses are made from some of the millions of tyres that are thrown away by motorists each year. The hose can be used on top of the soil but it probably distributes the water more widely if it is partially or fully buried. It can also be used under mulch material. If you are using water containing clay particles, a filter will be needed because the clay particles may cause blockages in the hose wall.

IN POTS
You can insert a section of coiled holey hose, blocked at one end, into a large pot of tomatoes. This is an ideal way to water tomatoes in a pot without getting the leaves wet.

Soaker Hoses

These are inflatable, semi-circular, thin-walled hoses which are blocked off at one end. They have small holes in the upper surface, through which fine jets of water spray in a gentle arch. They are not so good for tomatoes as they may wet the foliage. To keep the spray away from the foliage you can erect a wall of shade cloth or some such material near the plants, but it is probably easier to use another irrigation method. Some gardeners have complained that the material used in these hoses has a short life and needs to be treated kindly; if kinks develop, cracks may appear, so make sure they are rolled up and stored correctly after use.

Sprinklers

Sprinklers can be fixed or moveable, often with moving parts that spray water in a regular or segmented pattern. They are usually attached to the end of the hose and are great for lawns, seedling beds and most vegetables. However, they drench the foliage of tomato plants every time they are used and some wastage of water by evaporation does occur. A barrier may help but it is probably easier not to use sprinklers.

Microjets and Microsprays

These tiny water outlets are directed at individual plants. They are similar to trickle outlets (below) except that a higher pressure of water is needed and extra fine water filters are used. The microjets are particularly useful as they direct a small fan of water around the immediate root zone of the plant. A lot of water may be wasted from microjets and microsprays during very hot windy weather but they work well in sheltered gardens.

Trickle and Drip Irrigation

Rated by many as the best system for watering tomato plants, these consist of various types of microtubes (tiny tubes) stuck into a polythene pipe wherever they are needed. They allow water to drip out at a set rate, creating wet patches around the root area of plants, and are, therefore, very economical with water. However, when using this system it is wise to flush the tomato patch every few weeks with lots of water from a hand-held hose to prevent the build-up of salts within the soil around the wetted zone, especially if saline water from a bore is being used.

A coarse filter should be fitted near the tap outlet to filter large particles from the water, avoiding microtube blockages. Filters are often sold with the hose and tubing as kits. Regular checks on the drip line are also necessary because wasps and other insects or material can block the holes. The newer outlets are designed to be self-cleansing and need very little maintenance.

When using trickle or drip irrigation it is wise to attach a filter. Simple ones like this can be fitted near the outlet tap.

Install a small water tank to catch all run-off water from roofed areas. This can then be used on tomato plants.

The following systems water your plants while you're away.

Self-watering Systems

Hydroponic Watering Systems

In hydroponic systems gardeners can grow tomatoes in pots, troughs or guttering, the advantage of these systems is that they can be made fully automatic, allowing people to go on holiday for extended periods. Many of the systems are convenient and compact and can be placed inside the house, on a balcony, inside a greenhouse or along the wall of a house in an out of the way place. Hydroponic methods vary: some have a continuous flow, some use mist sprays, others just flood then drain the root area of plants at set intervals of time. Systems include the self-watering pot and the wick system (see p. 36 for further details).

Open-ended Containers

Some gardeners sink plant pots which are open-ended containers with small drainage holes, in the soil near their tomato plants and fill these when watering. The water gradually spreads underground to the root system of the plants. Water-filled collapsible bags with small holes can also be placed in a circle around plants, and these gradually leak water into the soil.

Beer Bottles

A variation on the above method is to use empty bottles. Fill them with water, leaving a small air gap at the top. Loosen the soil near the tomato plants, invert the bottle (holding your finger over the top), then jam it into the loose soil as you remove your finger. The contents will slowly drain out over a long period of time.

Water-saving Techniques

Installing Water Tanks

One of the most under-utilised methods of collecting water is to install small tanks to collect it from the roof. Millions of megalitres run off house roofs and into stormwater drains every year. Many home gardeners believe that house water tanks are not permitted in built-up areas, but this regulation only applies in some places. Most cities now allow the collection of rainwater in tanks and organisations such as city water boards actively encourage their use.

The water collected from roofs is perfectly safe for use on the garden but, often, not fit for human consumption until it has been filtered or has had further treatment because of the fallout from toxic air pollution and deposits from substances like soot and ash. Clean water can be obtained by flushing the roof regularly and keeping the run-off away from the collecting tank until it runs clean. Flow to the tank can then resume.

There are many small, well designed tanks available that are made from various materials. Some of these have self-flushing devices so they don't collect polluted run-off water.

Mulch on Mulch

Another way to conserve water is to mulch heavily on high-mounded garden beds and to place mulch in the pathways between each of the beds. The material in the pathways gradually composts and at the end of the season can be placed back on the garden beds to build them up again.

These beds only need watering once or twice a week in dry weather. One method of watering the mulched beds is to lay long pipes with large holes drilled along them horizontally through the centre of each bed. Each outlet hole should have hessian or old carpet wrapped around it to prevent the water from spurting. The water will percolate quickly through the material into the mulched beds, preventing salt deposits from buiding up and allowing the mulch to remain moist for long periods of time.

Waste Washing Water

Provided that biodegradable soaps are used, the water from clothes washing can be used for plants. Ideally, it should be diluted with pure water or diluted with normal water from the garden tap, because excessive use of soapy water may cause damage to plants due to the high level of soluble salts. An ideal combination is a 50:50 tank water and washing water mix accompanied by a thorough soaking with uncontaminated water at regular intervals.

3.4 Warmth and Protection

Tomatoes are warm-climate plants. They need plenty of protection from cool winds, frost and low ground temperatures, especially when they are seedlings. They will continue to fruit and survive at daytime temperatures between 18°C (65°F) and 30°C (86°F). However, they show symptoms of cold damage when subjected to prolonged temperatures at 0°C (32°F) or lower, and temperatures above 30°C (86°F) will inhibit the fruit set of most cultivars. Many of the small cherry-like tomato cultivars are likely to survive longer than the other types in cool areas. Although they can withstand slightly lower temperatures at night, they need some warmth to be able to set fruit (about 21°C/70°F for early-season tomatoes and about 25°C/77°F for mid-season tomatoes).

During the last few years, unusual climatic variation over the spring and summer has upset the normal growing habits of plants. To protect them from the unpredictable weather, some of which may be associated with the greenhouse effect, gardeners are finding that they need to use heating structures and greenhouses. The smaller ones used for seedlings should be partially lifted or removed entirely once the tomato plants have outgrown the structure.

There are several types of growing structures and greenhouses that can be used for raising seedlings and for growing mature tomato bushes. Some can easily be constructed using recycled plastic and/or bits of old wood or glass. Commercial mini-greenhouses that are lightweight and portable are available, so you can pop them on your tomatoes like a jacket when it's cold or (with some) use them to keep the area around the tomatoes moist when it gets too hot and dry.

Cheap Heating Using Recycled Materials

Bubble plastic (such as that used for packaging) or rigid double-walled plastic can be used to cover pots, propagating trays or plants.

An in-ground tomato plant that has been covered with bubble plastic supported by stakes and then covered completely with a plastic bag to trap all the warmth. This double layered plastic greenhouse system is also recommended for potted plants.

COVERING A POTTED TOMATO PLANT

Plastic Structures

1 Place two small bamboo sticks or a wire hoop inside the pot.
2 Place a plastic bag over the whole pot, so that the bag is held up by the supports away from the foliage, and tie the bag.
3 To provide warmth and retain heat, place a second bag over the first bag, tie and seal. This provides two layers of plastic with an air gap inside; the air gap acts as an insulation layer that traps the heat.

The pot is now a sealed system like a mini-terrarium and can be left unwatered for three to five weeks at a time. Do not place it in direct sunlight. A position under shade cloth or beneath trees or shrubs which receives morning sun or mottled shade is ideal.

Cupboard Capers

Tomatoes can be kept warm in pots inside a totally enclosed cupboard or building and fed by hydroponic systems (see chapter 2.3). The environment must be controlled with suitable heating and cooling apparatus and special plant lights used for about 16 hours each day to ensure adequate growth. Pollination is done by hand (see p. 17). This system is very suitable for people living in a fully enclosed flat or unit or in very cold climates where tomatoes can't be grown in the open garden.

Glass Pane System

Tomato seedlings in pots can be placed at the side of a building where they will receive morning sunlight and then plate glass windows leant over them. The sides are closed in with cardboard, timber, plastic or some other material. The plants may be kept under the glass until warm weather arrives and then planted out into the garden or left in pots without the glass protection.

Timber Protection

To provide a warmer environment, Italian and Chinese tomato growers often put boards or timber on the cool side (south side in the southern hemisphere) of planted seedlings in the field. The wood absorbs the sun's heat during the day and reflects it back at the tomatoes at night. Also, the wood shelters the plants from the wind. Alternatively, gardeners can closely plant other shrubs or trees near the tomatoes to protect the seedlings.

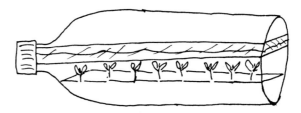

HOW CHILDREN CAN MAKE A GREENHOUSE WITH RECYCLED BOTTLES

A recycled see-through plastic bottle with the lid still on can be used to make an instant greenhouse for seedlings. This is a quick and easy and requires no maintenance between seed sowing and transplanting.

1. Using a knife and secateurs, cut along one side of the bottle and force it half open.
2. Place seedling mix into one side of the bottle which is lying on its side.
3. Moisten the mix.
4. Place a strip of paper towelling impregnated with tomato seeds (see p. 12) on the mix, and cover it with a thin sprinkle of mix.
5. Water the towelling with a liquid seaweed product.
6. Close the bottle up again, sealing it with masking tape or glue.
7. Place the bottle in a spot where it will receive some light but not full sun.
8. In winter, extra warmth can be created inside the bottle if it is enclosed in a sealed plastic bag or wrapped within a sheet of bubble plastic.
9. Leave the container alone for two to four weeks until the seedlings appear.
10. Open up the bottle to harden off the seedlings for a few days before transplanting them into the open garden or into pots.

Simple greenhouses made from recycled plastic bottles. Whole bottles can be used (see above) or half bottles can be placed over seed beds. The half bottles also protect the seedlings from slugs, snails and grubs.

Hydronurture greenhouses with water-filled walls enable tomato plants to grow quickly and produce early crops.

Commercial Heating Systems

The following are commercial heating aids that are ideal for raising tomato seedlings.

Heated Mats

Heated propagation blankets or mats can be placed at the base of seedling trays or pots.

Propagating Units

Propagation units with internal heating components (embedded electrical wires) are commonly used by gardeners. Some propagation units have a rigid plastic cover to increase humidity and prevent excessive loss of moisture during seed germination and the early stages of growth. To make the units warmer you can use solar-heated pipes (see p. 66). They also help to prevent the seed drying out or becoming too wet.

Water-filled Cells

A mini-greenhouse called Hydronurture has two great features: a double wall of plastic and long cell-like partitions that are filled with water. At first, when the seedlings have just been planted the cells are only partially filled with water and the igloo forms an almost-closed teepee around the plants. Both the double wall and the water retain and/or give off heat.

This system will develop strong plants that fruit early and will protect any basil plants that have been planted as companions near the tomato, allowing the basil to grow quickly with the extra warmth provided. The water in the walls may actually freeze, but when the ice starts to melt it gives off heat to the inner environment. Alternatively, during heatwaves these structures can actually help keep the plant environment moist and prevent burning.

When the weather warms and the tomato plants start to grow out of the top of the teepee the walls can be completely filled with water to allow more space.

Bubble Plastic Teepees

Bubble-plastic teepees (produced by Suncell Plant Guard) provide as much protection to young tomato plants as the water-filled cells but will not keep the plant environment as moist during summer.

Recycled Plastic

There is a windowsill-sized mini-greenhouse produced by Yates and made from recycled plastic. It has three vents, some mini-pots and is designed to hold a standard nursery punnet with eight plants. It also has an internal tray which can be compressed to aid removal of the pots.

Igloo Tunnels

Igloo tunnels can be erected over tomatoes in open beds. They are built by stretching clear plastic sheeting over hoop-shaped piping, hooped wires or bamboo and burying the edges in the soil. Recycled plastic bags can be used to make small tunnels. If another set of hoops is placed near the outside of the tunnel and another plastic cover put over the first to create an air gap, heat will be retained within the structure.

Greenhouses

Covering Materials

Plastic sheeting, bubble plastic, corflute (corrugated plastic that looks like cardboard), double-walled rigid plastic and glass materials can all be used for covering greenhouses. There are many forms of plastic sheeting, including coloured sheeting, sheeting to reduce radiation loss and reinforced materials suitable for wind-prone areas. Many home gardeners use just one layer of sheet plastic over a built frame to protect their early grown tomatoes from wind and cold. If you live near a greenhouse warehouse, it would be a good idea to spend some time looking at the materials that are available and collect some ideas for building your own greenhouse.

Most plastics now contain ultraviolet light inhibitors which prevent rapid degradation of the material when exposed to sunlight and extend its life. Plastic sheeting usually lasts for three years before needing replacement, provided that the sheeting is securely fastened down and protected from direct contact with sharp edges and bare metal surfaces.

All colours except green can be used. Green material will prevent the plants receiving some of the red light spectrum and thus stunt their growth.

Temperature

Recent research with growing tomatoes has shown that the ideal temperature inside a greenhouse at night is 10 to 14°C (50 to 57°F) and during the day 22 to 24°C (70 to 76°F) with a relative humidity of about 75 per cent.

EXTRA HEAT

In warm and tropical climates there is rarely any need for heating the greenhouse but heat may be needed in areas where there is frost at night.

SOLAR HEATING

You can also use permaculture gardening principles to warm up greenhouses or propagating units. Black drums filled with water will absorb

Yates produces a mini-greenhouse (for seedlings) made from recycled plastic. These seedlings were wilted before they were put into the mini-greenhouse, but now they are making a speedy recovery.

Simple greenhouses can be made by using plastic sheeting stretched over wire hoops and tied or buried at both ends and along the edges to create an enclosed growing frame.

heat during the day and their warmth will heat the greenhouse (or propagating unit). Water-filled black plastic piping fixed to the under-side of the roof will do the same thing.

BUBBLE PLASTIC AND THERMAL HEATING
Another way to conserve heat in a greenhouse, is to make a false roof of bubble plastic at head height. Sheet plastic or a thermal screen can also be used to completely cover the inside of the house. These materials act as thermal blankets and will greatly improve heat retention and reduce heating costs.

Shading in Greenhouses

Tomatoes in greenhouses need shade (and ventilation) during the hot summer months so that they don't become too hot. To provide shade:
- Various shade cloth materials giving different percentages of shading (e.g. 40 per cent, 50 per cent, 70 per cent) are available. Woven shade cloth and solar blanket materials, although much more expensive, are less likely to rip and tear and, if secured well, will last up to 20 years. Sheets of hessian or recycled webbing material placed over or next to the plants provides the cheapest form of shade.
- Use a moveable thermal screen in the greenhouse that can be pulled across at night and during extremely hot days. A thermal screen will reduce the day temperature significantly and increase the night temperature by up to 5°C (41°F), effectively preventing plant damage.

A Cheap Greenhouse Using Recycled Glass

Because of the cost of buying a glass-covered structure many gardeners may like to emulate Mr Jim Moore of Merbein, Victoria. He built his own glasshouse from differently sized recycled window-panes and glass doors for almost no cost. Jim took a long time working out how to fit the pieces together, but ended up with a very cheap and efficient glasshouse.

Organic Methods of Heating

Heat can be created by composting organic materials such as grass and manure, which, as they decompose, create heat. Seeds and seedlings placed above the decomposing materials will be kept warm. For various ways of doing this see p. 5 and p. 9.

Jim Moore of Merbein built this greenhouse entirely from recycled windowpanes. All the panes were different shapes, so the greenhouse design had to be adjusted as it was being built. The result is a very cheap efficient greenhouse.

Covering materials and the construction of greenhouses vary. One Italian home gardener created this special plastic-covered 'umbrella' greenhouse for his tomato plants.

4 Problems, Diseases and Pests

This fruit is infected with spotted wilt and cucumber mosaic virus, giving the unusual pattern and colour. The flesh is also thickened and dry, typical of some viral infections.

4.1 Problems

What follows is a description of some common problems, the results of which are often mistaken for a pest or disease. When you are working out the reason it is best to eliminate these problems before reaching for the the spray-gun!

General

Blossom Drop

Blossom drop can be caused by a number of factors, including the following:

- ☙ Heat stress accompanied by lack of water or food causing plants to go into survival mode.
- ☙ A sudden sharp change or drop in temperature— by 10 to 20°C (50 to 68°F)—causing plants to go into survival mode.
- ☙ Poor light (too little light getting to the plant) causing stress.
- ☙ Too much nitrogen fertiliser or manure will cause plants to switch to growth mode and produce leaves rather than flowers. Don't give your plants too much nitrogen before they start cropping. Add potassium.
- ☙ Very hot or cold water used for spraying.
- ☙ Chemical spray in a concentrated form and not at the recommended rate.
- ☙ Chemical pollution or accidental exposure or drenching with various chemicals.
- ☙ Lack of pollination.
- ☙ Animals and insects eating some of the floral parts of the tomato bush.
- ☙ Thrip activity.

Failure to Set Fruit

Fruit set is related to blossom drop, but pollination is also important. Factors such as very high temperatures and very cold temperatures have a direct effect on pollination and lack of pollination will cause failure of the crop. Pollination is usually done by bees and other insects as they transfer pollen from one flower to the next, or by the wind. If no insects are available, pollination and fruit set will not occur unless aided in some way.

Tomato leaves showing severe wilt due to 40°C (104°F) day temperatures. These leaves returned to rigidity approximately 10 minutes after being watered. Tomato plants, especially those grown in pots, may need watering two or three times daily during extremely hot weather.

Heat Stress Wilt

Tomato leaves subjected to really hot dry conditions actually 'close down', lose moisture and droop. The stomata (breathing holes in the leaf surface) close up so that transpiration and respiration ceases. This is an emergency system that allows the plant to survive a hostile environment. During times of heat stress, blossom end rot (see p. 13) may also start. Gardeners will find that after the heat stress period is over, the plant's leaves return to turgidity and function normally.

This tomato plant shows the typical leaf distortion, curling and lack of leaf formation due to pollutants.

Pollutants
Tomato plants react quickly to any chemical pollutants in the soil or the air. The signs include: a mass distortion of growth, puckered leaves, yellowing blotchy leaves, miniaturisation of leaves, fan-like growth of leaflets or gradual death of whole plants. If any hormones used in animal feed remain in the manure the plants will show severely distorted growth patterns. Composting contaminated manure for several weeks before giving it to the plants will usually break down the pollutants. The sensitivity of the tomato plant enables it to be used as an indicator plant when judging whether the environment or soil is healthy.

Sunburnt Fruits and Leaves
If tomatoes are subjected to too much heat and sunlight, whitish, yellow or yellowy white patches appear on the skin. Severe burns can also cause a hard, grey, blistered centre to develop within the burn area. If tomatoes are not fully protected by leafy shade, they will burn during dry hot weather if the plant is under water stress especially during unseasonal weather conditions, for example a 40°C (104°F) blustery hot dry day. Sunburn may also occur if the plants have lost foliage cover due to

Both the leaves and fruits of tomatoes can be severely burnt. Shadecloth or some partial shaded area is necessary when temperatures reach 40°C (104°F).

  ♨ diseases such as blight
  ♨ insect attack
  ♨ plants wilting
  ♨ gardeners pruning too severely
When tomatoes are growing in igloos or glasshouses under hot conditions, without humidity, fruit can also burn.

To prevent this condition make sure the plant's shade and moisture requirements are met and provide high humidity around the foliage during hot dry periods. Gardeners can erect partial shade barriers with materials such as shade cloth to give protection during the hot afternoon period, or plant tomatoes near garden trees or shrubs that will give partial shading. Growing climbing beans, choko, passionfruit vines or other fruit-producing plants on the sunny side of the tomato patch would also be a good idea. See p. 66 for more information on shading in a greenhouse.

Fruit

Birds and Rats

In these days of bird conservation the invasion of garden dwelling birds into the vegetable patch is common. Birds usually eat or partially eat fruit just as it is ripening.

Use bird-proof netting or place paper bags around the ripening fruit to prevent damage occurring.

Rats may be a problem in some areas. They always seem to eat the tomato the night before you intended to pick it and will eat whole fruit or tear strips out of its side. Once they have found a food source they will continue to visit.

Use rat traps, cover fruit just before ripening, or place tomato plants in a rat-proof, caged area.

Rats can chew the fruit of tomatoes just as it is becoming ripe for picking. Rat traps or pet cats may be the only answer to this problem.

Catface

This common name refers to an unusual pattern of markings that appear on some tomato fruits. The fruit may become unusually large, or just have scar-like marks crisscrossing the skin surface. If the marks are examined closely, they look like stitch marks. There is usually some disfiguring of the fruit. Crazy face-like fruit are often formed due to uneven bulging growth between the scar lines on the skin. One theory is that catface conditions are brought on during cool weather at flowering time when some pollen may stick to the small, developing, sensitive young fruits causing the skin markings. It is mainly a physiological condition and no remedial action is required; all fruit affected are quite edible. Catfacing may also be enhanced by a slight virus or mycoplasma infection within the plant, for example big bud virus (see p. 76).

Sometimes tomato fruits form unbelievable face-like structures as is shown in this picture.

Cracks

Radial cracks will occur on fully ripe or ripening tomatoes when they are subjected to rain or water from overhead sprinkling systems during hot weather. Growth cracks may also occur while the green tomato fruit is actively growing; these usually show around the circumference of the tomato. Some tomato varieties are more susceptible than others to cracking of the fruit. To reduce the incidence of this condition, make sure that there is no moisture stress and provide partial shade and shelter to ensure adequate leaf protection of the fruit from the hot sun. An adequate nutrient supply with emphasis on micro-nutrients and calcium is also important. Micro-nutrients can be supplied by foliar sprays, such as liquid seaweeds and mineral

Cracks can allow rots to get in or cause the fruit to grow one-sided, as in this case. Reducing overhead watering, providing adequate nutrition and shading of fruits will prevent cracks from occurring.

fertilisers, or by trace elements applied to the soil. Apply foliar sprays in the early morning to allow the leaves to dry before nightfall and reduce leaf infections. A supply of calcium to the plant to strengthen cell walls is also important. Gardeners must make sure they harvest the fruit as it ripens because there are a number of pests and diseases that will take advantage of the cracks.

Misshapen

Crooked, elongated, bumpy or misshapen fruits can be caused by problems already mentioned, for example, big bud and catface. Crooked fruit can be the result of unevenly set seed within the fruit, genetic or structural change brought on by insect damage, chemical damage, genetic mutation of a few cells within the fruit, or abnormal and incomplete fertilisation where few, if any, seeds form but the fruit develops fully. Do not save seed from crooked fruits.

Puffiness

Some tomato cultivars have puffy and dry flesh, often developing open cavities similar to the related capsicum fruits. This condition can be caused by varietal differences, hormone sprays, or nutrient deficiencies. Some gardeners choose these types specially for filling with other food before cooking and have named them 'stuffing tomatoes'.

Green Tomatoes

Many gardeners are unaware that some of the old heritage tomato varieties such as 'Greenwich' and 'Green Zebra' have green fruits when ripe.

Leaves

Inrolled

Often this condition is seen on hard-pruned plants and plants that have been subjected to **too much water**. The leaves will grow thick and leathery, but brittle, and show an inward turning leaf roll. This usually starts at the lower end of the plant and progresses upwards. Geneticists have found that some varieties are more subject to inrolled leaves than others and that the condition is of genetic origin, causing no harm or reduced fruit production from the plants affected.

Misshapen tomato fruit is caused by uneven seed set and catface (see p. 71).

Inrolling of the leaf was once thought to be a result of virus infection, but it is a condition occurring naturally within certain cultivars and varieties.

4.2 Diseases

Diseases often attack plants because they are unhealthy or sickly or susceptible to a disease. They may be spread in many ways including handling, tools, wind, rain, overhead watering, spores, infected soil or seed, insects, animals, dust or by grafting. Other factors such as climate, temperature, moisture, air movement and nutrient supply contribute to disease build-up.

Apply a copper-based fungicidal dust or spray such as Bordeaux.

Apply a sulphur-based fungicidal dust or spray to kill spores, some diseases and as a dust to control mites.

Avoid careless handling, firstly, to prevent damage that will invite infection and, secondly, because bacteria ooze from the infected areas and therefore the disease is easily spread or carried by brushing infected foliage, handling plants, or by rain or splashed water dripping through the plants.

Avoid overhead watering to reduce the spreading by splashing of disease spores.

Be hygienic, washing tools and hands to minimise the spread of diseases. Do not handle infected material and then touch another tomato plant.

Clean the mix (see p. 8).

Clean the seeds using one of the three methods described on p. 11–12.

Control insect attacks see the summary of methods on pp. 79–80.

Control thrips which may transfer diseases or rasp away and destroy floral parts and leaf surfaces.

Control weeds to stop the insect population increasing, prevent cross-infection of viruses and to reduce root competition around the plants.

Grow plants in a hot dry place so they don't become waterlogged or over wet. You still need to water well.

Improve drainage by raising beds or laying agricultural drains. Add sand or bulky material to the potting mix.

Improve plant health by using organic fertilisers, mulches, liquid seaweed sprays and granules, lime to provide cell-building calcium and moisture to prevent plants suffering stress.

Introduce companion plants to reduce disease attack.

Let the the soil lie fallow to interupt the life cycle of pests or diseases.

Plant in pots (see chapter 2.2)

Provide shelter from the sun so that the fruit doesn't burn and split, allowing bacteria to enter the cracks.

Prune to allow plenty of light and air penetration into the middle of the plant. This will also improve air flow and allow quick drying of the wetted foliage after rain.

Remove infected parts of the plant and hot compost (see p. 53) or destroy this material to prevent the spread of disease.

Remove infected plants and burn.

Rotate crops (a four-year rotation is usually the norm) to reduce the build-up of disease organisms in the soil.

Use disease-resistant cultivars or rootstocks to overcome certain disease problems (see chapter 1.3 or the charts at the back of the book).

Key to Organic Prevention/ Control Methods

Use lime to provide calcium and prevent blossom end rot.
Water regularly to prevent water stress.

> A new biological product Trichopel (pellets containing *Tricho-derma* species of fungi) may soon be available to home gardeners. Using these naturally occurring saprophytic fungi helps control some soil disease organisms, increases the growth of tomato seedlings and allows plants to produce larger crops by initiating better nutrient supply to the roots of the plants.

Bacterial Diseases

Bacterial Canker (Claribacter michigenensis subsp. michigenensis) or 'Birds-eye Spot'

The bacterium causing this disease lives in the soil. It enters the plant system by attacking the soft tissue found just under the stem bark and then by infecting roots or stems. It can infect seed, seedlings, leaves and fruit of tomato plants and is usually common when tomatoes are grown under glass or in greenhouses, but can also be a problem if plants are grown in open beds.

Symptoms: Leaflets will wilt at the edge. Leaves will turn a light brown colour, wither and die, but remain firmly attached to the plant. Terminal shoots may wither and die after nearly all the foliage has been affected. Whitish grey to greyish brown streaks may appear on the stems or leaf stalks and these can become brittle and crack open to form cankers. Once infected, cut stems will show a yellow discoloration. Often the disease attacks leaflets on one side of the leaf only, so that half the leaflets become brown and dead, and half still remain green and healthy looking. The disease travels upwards through the plant and bacteria spread or splashed upon the fruit cause white spots on the skin which later show a slightly raised, brown, roughened growth. The white colour around the spot remains, resulting in the disease symptoms being given the common name 'birds-eye spot'.

Prevention/Control: Apply a copper-based fungicidal dust or spray, avoid overhead watering, improve drainage, remove infected parts, remove infected plants, rotate crops. Don't use infected fruit as a seed.

Bacterial Speck (Pseudomonas syringae pv tomato)

Infection usually occurs during periods of high humidity and low temperatures (18 to 24°C/64 to 75°F).

Symptoms: Small dark brown to black spots appear on the green tomato fruit and leaves, giving them a speckled look; ripening fruit seem resistant to this disease. It can also cause the leaves to have a darker green colour around the spots, almost like a halo. Infected seedlings have a tendency to lose vigour. Severe infections are evident when there are large numbers of spots on the leaves and the tissue around the infected area turns yellow. Often infected fruit only show one or a few tiny spots on the skin, so look carefully before saving fruits for seed.

Prevention/Control: Rotate crops, apply a copper-based fungicidal dust or spray, remove infected plants.

Bacterial canker.

Bacterial speck can cause black spots to occur on tomato fruits. These fruit are suitable for eating but should not be kept for seed unless given heat treatment as the disease is seed-borne.

Symptoms: Small lesion areas appear under the leaves. At first these appear as brownish grey spots. Infection of stalks and fruit may produce brown-black water-soaked spots and severe infection at flowering can cause the flowers to drop. Fruit may develop raised blistered areas that become rough scabby surfaces.

Prevention/Control: Apply a copper-based fungicidal dust or spray, avoid careless handling, clean the seed (any of the methods), control weeds, rotate crops.

Bacterial Spot (Xanthomonas campestris pv vesicatoria)

Several strains of this disease occur during cool weather and others occur during hot humid conditions. The disease is particularly annoying for home gardeners because the plant may be infected in its prime when lots of fruit are starting to ripen.

Symptoms: There are no external symptoms, the tomato plant just suddenly wilts. It can be healthy one day, but dead the next. Adventitious roots may appear on stems. Some plants seem to recover at night, only to wilt during the next day but these will eventually die. If the stems of the tomato plant at ground level are cut, a brown discoloration can be seen and, if this tissue is squeezed, a grey-white slimy material may ooze from the stem.

Prevention/Control: The only thing to do is to pull the plant out and make green chutney from the green tomatoes, or hang the plant up to allow some of the fruit to ripen. Be hygienic, clean the seed (any of the methods), rotate crops.

Bacterial Wilt (Pseudomonas solanacearum)

There are lots of virus diseases that attack tomato plants. The organisms are so minute they can only be seen with an electron microscope. They live in individual plant cells. Symptoms vary from no evidence of infection to severe plant distortion, fruit and leaf colouring or speckling and stunting of plants. Severe infections by some viruses can cause plant decline or death. Viruses are transferable from a host plant to the tomato, and host plants may include weeds and other vegetables. Many plants survive mild infestations while some plants succumb to three or more virus infestations at once and rapidly decline.

Viruses

Symptoms: A general mottling of the leaves is usual but some tomato plants severely infected with this virus show massive distortion of the leaves, with abnormally thin narrow leaflets and very little green tissue.

Prevention/Control: Be hygienic, clean the seed (hot water treatment), remove infected plants. Also, control sucking insects.

Cucumber Mosaic Virus

This disease is particularly damaging during cool weather periods in early spring or summer. There are several host plants that carry it, including the Australian ground cover plant *Brachycome* species.

Symptoms: There can be two stages of infection.

1 Bronze or chocolate-coloured markings on leaflets.
2 A tip blight causing drooping of the shoots and cessation of growth.
Agate-like concentric-ringed blotches of yellow and red may also develop on the fruits. Sometimes the blotchy fruit fails to ripen properly, but it can still be eaten.

Spotted Wilt (caused by tomato spotted wilt virus (TSWV))

Plants rarely die but will become dwarfed. Some tomato cultivars that recover from the first infection go on to produce bunchy growth and can develop purplish tints under the leaves and on young shoots and stems (these symptoms are the same as acute potash deficiency).

Prevention/Control: Control thrips, control weeds, remove infected plants.

Tomato Big Bud (caused by Phytoplasma *organism)*

Big bud is spread by leaf hoppers which move from weeds such as black nightshade, capeweed, fat hen, kangaroo apple and mustard. The insects are usually active during midsummer and virus-like symptoms rarely occur before this time.

Symptoms: Shoots are spike-like because the leaves are not fully developed and show a bluish or purplish or yellowish tinge on the new growth. Floral parts can become greenish, distended, fused and swollen, or form multiple shoots. Fruit developing from the infected buds have hard woody flesh. A single flower within a group of flower buds may develop the disease and have a flattened calyx and stem, fused buds and enlarged sepals that look like a green daisy flower.

Prevention/Control: Control leaf hoppers by using an insecticidal dust or spray or using sticky traps. Control weeds, remove infected parts.

Tomato Mosaic Virus and Tobacco Mosaic Virus

These two viruses are together because of the similar symptoms they produce. It can also infect several weed species which can help spread the disease.

Symptoms: These vary with different strains of the virus, it can cause light or dark green or bright yellow mottling of the leaves and puckering malformation of the leaflets. Stunting of the plants and some fruit mottling has also been observed. Cross-infection can occur through plants touching one another, or during gardening operations such as pruning, picking, tying and transplanting.

Prevention/Control: Control weeds, rotate crops, hygiene, remove infected parts. DON'T SMOKE!

Fungal Diseases

Anthracnose (Colletotrichum atramentarium)

Symptoms: Depressed circular spots on ripening fruit, dark markings on seedling stems and leaves. The circular spots may develop into spreading concentric rings with black dots in the centre that produce pink spores during warm humid weather.

This tomato fruit is infected with tomato mosaic virus.

With tomato big bud virus, the buds may fuse and become enlarged, spreading sideways like a fan. Sometimes, removal of the infected shoot will get rid of the problem but the virus may infect the whole plant and in those cases it should be pulled out and destroyed.

Prevention/Control: Apply a copper-based fungicidal dust or spray, improve drainage, remove infected parts, rotate crops.

This is common in both commercial and home gardens crops.
Symptoms: Stem tissue of young tomato plant seedlings wilts and sometimes dies. It is common in early spring during cool weather conditions when plants are more subject to disease attack.
Prevention/control: Apply a copper-based fungicidal dust or spray, clean the seed (any method). Also, thin seedlings that are too close together to provide air circulation and avoid excessive watering.

Damping Off (usually caused by the fungus Pythium *spp. and* Rhizoctonia solani)

It is mainly active when there are spring and early summer rains. Crops protected under glass or in igloos will not develop the disease easily. In dry inland areas with dry hot summers the disease is not prevalent.
Symptoms: Small jagged brown spots occur mainly on older leaves. These enlarge (to about 1 cm/½ in) and marks like concentric rings appear, not unlike 'bullseye' markings, within the damaged area. With severe infestations whole leaves may be spotted and turn yellow. Fruit may also be attacked late in the season as it matures, causing sunken hard-skinned areas that may also show the typical target spot concentric circles. Tissue damage may extend deeply into the fruit
Prevention/Control: Apply a copper- or sulphur-based fungicidal dust or copper spray, avoid overhead watering, improve plant health, remove infected parts, use disease-resistant cultivars or rootstocks.

Early Blight (Alternaria solani)

This occurs during the hot summer months and only attacks tomato plants.
Symptoms: Drooping and wilting of the lower leaves, eventually spreading upwards until the whole plant wilts then dies. The fungus moves throughout the inner tissue of the stem causing a brown discoloration which can be seen if infected plant stems are cut and examined. Young tomato seedlings can be attacked and die from damping off.
Prevention/Control: Be hygienic, clean the mix, clean the seed (hot water treatment), remove infected parts, rotate crops, use disease-resistant cultivars or rootstocks.

Fusarium Wilt (Fusarium oxysporum sp. lycopersici)

mping off can cause sudden collapse of tomato seedling stem so that it falls r. Using clean trays and pasteurised or ʳilised seedling mixes will solve this blem.

Tomato leaves showing the symptoms of early blight. With severe infection these lesions will cover more of the leaf surface.

The cross-sectioned root system of a tomato plant showing the internal browning caused by fusarium wilt. Death of the root will follow.

Grey Mould
(Botrytis cinerea)

This is a post-harvest rot infecting flowers and small developing fruitlets.
Symptoms: The plant part affected develops a grey hairy growth on the surface.
Prevention/Control: No organic controls available. Just use a commercial fungicide.

Late Blight
(Phytophthora
infestans)

This fungus also infects potato crops and is called Irish blight. It is prevalent during periods of muggy warm humid weather when cool nights are also experienced.
Symptoms: The disease causes blackened greasy areas to appear on the leaves, often along the leaf margins. Eventually the whole leaf may be infected and, in humid conditions, a grey mould can be seen on the underside. Immature or ripe fruit may be infected and show a discoloured, hardened, corkyness of the surface tissue which rots. Fruits showing no symptoms at harvest may show extensive breakdown when stored.
Prevention/Control: Use other controls as listed for early blight. Also, ensure warm dry air environment.

Powdery Mildew
(Oidiopsis taurica)

Symptoms: Attacks mature leaves and shows as irregular blotchy diseased section that die in the centre; also yellowing around the infected area.
Prevention/Control: Apply a sulphur-based fungicidal dust or spray, improve plant health, remove infected leaves.

Sclerotinia Stem
Rot

Several species of the fungus *Sclerotinia* can cause this disease during cool wet weather conditions when aeration within the plants is poor.
Symptoms: Rotting of the lower stem. This may be followed by black fungal spores developing inside the pithy part of the tomato plant stems.
Prevention/Control: Apply a copper-based fungicidal dust or spray, improve drainage, plant in pots, prune, remove infected parts.

Soft Rots (caused
by both fungi and
bacterial organisms
e.g. Anthracnose,
Colletotrichum,
Penicillium,
Phoma, Rhizopus,
Sclerotinia *spp.)*

Fungal or bacterial rots may invade fruit that is soft and overripe, in contact with wet soil, or has sustained some sort of physical injury. An opening or crack allows organisms to enter the fruit. Ripened fruit is high in sugar that can supply disease organisms with food, so that the rots usually spread very quickly.
Symptoms: A partial rotting on the skin or within the fruit.
Prevention/Control: Apply a copper-based fungicidal dust or spray, avoid careless handling, improve plant health, provide shelter from the sun, prune, rotate crops, use lime, water regularly. Pick the fruit at the right stage because if it gets old it will get soft and might crack. Store the fruit in a well-ventilated, open, cool place.

Sooty Mould

This black fungal organism lives on the sugary exudations of insects, usually aphids or white fly, that infect the tomato plants.
Symptoms: A black sooty covering on leaves branches, twigs or fruit.
Prevention/Control: Apply a copper-based fungicidal dust or spray, control insect attacks.

Many soft rots can attack tomato fruits, especially when they are ripe. It is important to pick the fruit at the correct stage, handle without bruising and to store them properly.

Tomato leaves showing infestation of white flies. They exude a sticky substance that attracts the black sooty mould, shown here as black dots and smudges.

This fungus is prevalent during cool weather.

Symptoms: Plants wilt during warm or daylight periods, but recover at night to become turgid and healthy looking by morning. The disease gradually causes the lower leaves of the tomato plant to turn yellow and die; the plants will also eventually die. When the stems of infected plants are cut open, a brown discoloration can be seen extending along the core.

Prevention/Control: Clean the mix, control weeds, rotate crops, use disease-resistant cultivars or rootstocks.

Verticillium Wilt (Verticillium dahliae)

4.3 Pests

Pests range from minute tomato mites to large grubs, beetles and small animals. They can live underground, inside the plant or on it, fly in, be injected into or rubbed onto plants, and can bite, suck, chew, rasp or chomp away at the plants.

Apply Dipel (*Bacillus thuringiensis*), a bacterium that controls the larvae of many insects.

Apply an insecticidal dust or spray. Dusts containing derris or rotenone (both plant extracts) can be used for chewing insects and sprays such as pyrethrum (a plant extract), hot chillis, soapy water, Clensel, and oils to kill eggs.

Clean the mix but this is not practical for large amounts (see p. 8).

Collect by hand (use a torch at night).

Control weeds to stop the insect population increasing, prevent cross-infection of viruses and to reduce root competition around the plants.

Cover the fruit with paper bags just before it starts to colour and ripen.

Destroy egg masses, usually found on the underside of leaves, to help keep insect numbers down.

Key to Organic Prevention/Control Methods

Grow green manure crops to improve the soil and prevent disease build-up (see p. 49).

Grow plants in a hot dry place so they don't become waterlogged or over wet. You still need to water well.

Hang up sticky traps made from pieces of recycled cardboard or bought from plant nurseries. These attract insects such as thrips, white fly, aphids and ants and can be used to reduce the insect population.

Introduce animals such as ducks, geese or chickens to control certain insects.

Introduce companion plants to help keep down insects (see chapter 2.4).

Let the the soil lie fallow to interupt the life cycle of pests or diseases.

Place aluminium on the soil around the plants to scare away flying insects.

Plant in pots (see chapter 2.2).

Remove infected parts of the plant and hot compost (see p. 53) or destroy this material to prevent the spread of disease. This will also improve air flow and allow quick drying of the wetted foliage after rain.

Remove infected plants and burn.

Rotate crops (a four-year rotation is usually the norm) to reduce the build-up of disease organisms in the soil.

Use a water jet to kill soft-bodied insects.

Use insect-proof netting to prevent flying insects and pests from attacking plants.

Use organic insecticidal baits which are pot-like traps with insect attractants inside.

Aphids

Not generally injurious to garden-grown tomato plants, aphids can sometimes become a pest with tomatoes grown under cover or in greenhouses. As well as sucking sap from plants, they transmit viral diseases from one plant to another.

Symptoms: These sucking insects can be seen on drooping new leaves.

Prevention/Control: Apply an insecticidal dust or spray, introduce companion plants, place aluminium foil on the soil, use a water jet. Introduce ladybirds.

The larvae, which are curled whitish grubs, normally live in uncultivated soil feeding on the roots of grasses. When new areas are cleared for garden use this beetle may become a pest. The beetles are shiny black, about 12 mm (½ in) long and oval in shape.

Symptoms: The adult beetles (which hatch in spring) often chew the base of plants at ground level, severely damaging them.

Prevention/Control: Collect by hand, let the soil lie fallow. Flood the soil to make the beetles emerge.

Black African Beetle

The black field cricket is a shiny black or brown, very agile insect with grasshopper-like back legs. It breeds in cracks in the soil and can occur in vast numbers. It is about 25 mm (1 in) long.

Symptoms: Crickets eat foliage, chew holes in leaves and stems and demolish the growing tips of young seedlings, usually attacking them in autumn.

Prevention/Control: Prepare the garden area by using lots of compost and mulching heavily so that it is not suitable for crickets. Introduce animals, use organic insecticidal baits. Attract birds to the garden.

Black Cricket

The adults are 4 to 5 cm (1½ in) long, a brownish purple with triangular spots on each side of the body.

Symptoms: These caterpillars are not fussy about which plants they attack. Their name describes their feeding habits; they cluster together and feed on the underside of the leaves, skeletonising them.

Prevention/Control: If caught in the cluster stage, hundreds of insects can be destroyed by simply squashing. Apply an insecticidal dust or spray.

Cluster Caterpillar

Tomatoes are often infested with writhing tiny white maggots that can be mistaken for fruit fly larvae.

Symptoms: Usually they are found in fruit that has been injured or split or has rotted, providing an entry point for the adult fly to lay eggs. The eggs are tiny—2 to 3 mm (¹/₁₀ in) long—and greyish black. The main difference between fruit fly maggots and ferment fly maggots is that the ferment fly maggots, unlike fruit fly maggots, do not jump and flip in the air when they are touched lightly or prodded.

Prevention/Control: Destroy waste fruit and cover any stored, damaged fruit (i.e. fruit which is being kept to make sauce, paste or juice). Bury or hot compost spoiled fruit.

Ferment Flies

The adults are about 18 mm (¾ in) long, light brown to greyish brown or dark brown and may have white stripes along their side at the top.

Symptoms: Plague grasshopper swarms can suddenly fly in to eat and destroy tomato plants. When open fields dry off the insects sometimes move into home gardens and may feed on anything green.

Prevention/Control: Organic control of this insect is not easy; insect-proof netting may be used on some plants. A new organic material from the neem tree is being trialed and looks promising. This may be available to home gardeners within two to five years.

Grasshoppers (grasshopper nymphs or wingless grasshoppers)

Green Vegetable Bug

This insect sucks juice from plants and from developing fruit. The young bugs are round and orange and black. They then turn into multi-coloured forms. The adults are green and shield-shaped, but may become a dirty brown colour during winter. Full development from egg to adult takes between five to eight weeks so that huge populations can build up quickly. The bug overwinters in sheltered areas such as fences, wood piles, and behind boxes.

Symptoms: Affected parts may wilt and become retarded in growth. Tomato fruits that are attacked will develop sunken or hardened corky areas at the injury point.

Prevention/Control: Apply an insecticidal dust or insecticidal spray (this insect, however, is resistant to most chemical sprays), collect by hand, control weeds, destroy egg masses, use insect-proof netting.

Harlequin Bug

These bugs are about 12 mm (½ in) long and a brilliant black and reddish orange on top, with the underbelly a green-yellow and black colouring. These Australian insects can breed in large numbers in surrounding shrub and grassed areas, then invade crops during summer. They are easily noticed sucking juices from tomato plants, flowers and fruit.

Symptoms: As for the green vegetable bug.

Prevention/Control: As for the green vegetable bug.

Hawkmoths

There are many species of hawkmoths, all of which have distinctive larvae (grubs) with a protruding horn. The grubs are often very colourful, but well camouflaged; some have markings that look like eye spots on the body. They can be from 5 to 9 cm (2 to 4 in) in length. The adult moths have a characteristic delta wing shape and a torpedo-like body.

Symptoms: Because hawkmoth grubs are very large, they can eat a lot of one plant in a very short time, leaving green droppings at the base of plants attacked.

Prevention/Control: Apply Dipel, collect by hand, use insect-proof netting.

Heliothis Grub (also called budworms)

The grubs are about 25 to 30 mm (1 in) long and vary in colour from a bright pale green to a dark greenish brown with stripes along the body. Female moths lay single eggs on the foliage and buds of the tomato from the time of first flowering until cropping ceases. Each female may lay hundreds of eggs. The young caterpillars mature in two to four weeks then leave the plant and burrow in the soil to pupate.

Symptoms: Holes in buds, foliage and fruit. A mature grub burrows from one fruit to another and the resulting holes can be very large. They usually attack the tomatoes nearest ground level.

Prevention/Control: Collect by hand, apply an insecticidal dust or spray. Keeping foliage of plants off the ground will control numbers.

Jassids

Jassids look like miniature cicadas and can be brown or green. They are about 4 mm (⅛ in) long. They readily take flight when disturbed and move sideways when approached. Tomato plants are not a preferred host for this insect so it rarely builds up to numbers that are worrisome.

These tomatoes are being attacked by a green vegetable bug, which usually occurs in small numbers so that hand picking is the best control method to use but, beware, the juice of the squashed insect has a putrid smell.

The heliothis grub is a common sight in the tomato patch and a few grubs can ruin one crop. They are hard to see because they are often the same colour as the surrounding foliage. Hand picking the grubs from a few plants is the best method of control, but in large plantings dusts or sprays can be used.

Symptoms: Jassids suck juice from plants causing some leaves to yellow and fall.
Prevention/Control: Apply an insecticidal dust or spray, use insect-proof netting.

Leptocoris Bug

This bug is shield-shaped with a tan or reddish brown body and other markings; underneath the body is dark red and dark green. It is about 6 mm (¼ in) long. The adult is thin, narrow and shield-shaped with long, segmented, bent, black antennae. It is a widely distributed Australian insect.
Symptoms: Usually attacks fruit and sucks out the juices.
Prevention/Control: Collect by hand, control weeds.

Loopers

Loopers are often the same colour as the plant they are feeding on, so are very hard to find. They are also able to remain rigid like small twigs stuck at right angles to the branch or stem that they are on, giving them great camouflage.
Symptoms: These grubs form a bent loop when they move and feed on the plant foliage, making holes.
Prevention/Control: Apply an insecticidal dust or spray, collect by hand.

Metallic Green Tomato Fly

The adult insect is a shiny, dark, metallic green and about 6 mm (¼ in) long with the triangular shape of the Queensland fruit fly. The maggots are very similar to the Queensland fruit fly and are capable of springing when approached.

Symptoms: Unlike the Queensland fruit fly, they only lay eggs in tomato fruit that has already been split or injured as the female cannot inject eggs into the whole fruit.

Prevention/Control: Remove damaged fruit and pick fruit regularly so that it cannot become overripe.

Mole Cricket

This insect rarely appears in large numbers and often will attack tomato plants only when fresh ground has been prepared for cultivation.

Symptoms: Sometimes the stems of seedlings are chewed; more often the cricket dislodges a whole plant as it moves through the soil. Mole crickets live underground and often feed near the surface of the soil, leaving cracked uplifted earth where they have been burrowing.

Prevention/Control: This is usually unnecessary.

Potato Moth

The larvae of this moth usually attack potato plants but can cause problems with tomato plants if rogue or self-sown potato plants from the previous season are left growing with tomatoes.

Symptoms: The tiny caterpillar of the potato moth can mine into leaf stalks, stems or leaves, causing a blister-like brown patch on the leaf. The tiny pink larvae may also bore into the fruit, especially where two fruits touch one another.

Prevention/Control: Apply an insecticidal dust or spray, pull out any rogue or self-sown potato plants.

Queensland Fruit Fly

This fly attacks a large range of fruits and vegetables. The female lays eggs by depositing them through a needle-like tube into the fruit and they hatch into triangular jumping maggots.

Symptoms: The egg injection point usually seals up so that the only visible sign of infestation is a small dry black dot. The maggots can turn the whole of the inside of a fruit into a blackened mess and make it inedible.

Prevention/Control: Cover the fruit, use insect-proof netting, use organic insecticidal baits.

PAPAYA FRUIT FLY

> During October 1995 a newly introduced pest, which affects most fruit and vegetables, was discovered in Queensland. Control methods for this dangerous pest are as for the Queensland fruit fly.

Red Spider Mite

Spider mites, which cannot usually be seen with the naked eye, are very seldom found in large numbers on tomato leaves.

Symptoms: These tiny mites inhabit the underside of leaves and suck juices from the plant. Infected tomato leaves become whitish and mottled on the upper surface. With severe infestations, fine webbing

threads appear all over the foliage and the leaves will dry out, turn brown and then die.
Prevention/Control: Apply a sulphur dust or spray. Introduce predator mites.

These very tiny worm-like eelworms breed rapidly and can infest the soil within a short distance of the infected plant; this soil carried to other parts of the garden will spread the infestation. Eelworms have an enormous host range and can be found on many plants *Root Knot Nematodes (Eelworms)*

Symptoms: Eelworms feed on the roots of plants, entering the root tissue and causing lumps to form along the root system. This, in turn, limits the ability of the plant to obtain nutrients. Severely affected plants usually become stunted and the leaves turn yellow.
Prevention/Control: Chemical nematocides have been developed but . . . Control weeds, let the soil lie fallow, grow green manure crops, plant in pots, clean the mix.

These are small, grey, thin, shield-shaped bugs about 5 mm (¼ in) long and very active. They overwinter in weeds and breed on wild vegetation. *Rutherglen Bug*

Symptoms: They invade blossoms and can suck juices from plants and fruit.
Prevention/Control: Various natural biological control organisms exist (e.g. spiders), but these are not commercially available. Wet springs with heavy rain will reduce numbers. Very fine-meshed insect-proof netting can be used.

Root knot nematodes (eelworms) cause ball-like structures which impede the uptake of nutrients by the root system and make the plants remain small and unproductive.

Slugs and Snails

Symptoms: Slugs and snails attack young seedlings when they are juicy and tender, leaving holes in the leaves or destroying seedling tip growth.
Prevention/Control: Introduce animals, use organic insecticidal baits, collect by hand. Use a greenhouse bottle or some kind of plastic cover to protect the plant. A new, almost organic material is Multicrop's Multiguard pellets which contain an iron compound often found in mixed fertiliser. It is reputed to be very safe to use where there are birds and animals.

BEER TRAP

> To make a beer trap, buy a small plastic funnel or a deep plastic dish, cut the base off and place a small cork in the hole. Place one or several of these funnel shapes around the garden where the slugs and snails are active. Obtain some stale beer and place it in the funnel opening. Snails and slugs are attracted to the beer. Some drown, others lose their way and cook in the hot sun, and a few are picked up by birds.

Thrips

Young thrips are yellowish; they eventually turn a dark brown to black when the adult size of 2 to 3 mm ($^1/_{10}$ in) is reached. They breed on grasses during the early spring. When the host plants start drying off during early summer, they migrate, using the prevailing winds and invade home vegetable gardens and other plants often in plague numbers.
Symptoms: Thrips rasp away at the plant surface causing abrasions which colour after a period of time, giving the leaves a whitish or silvery appearance. Thrips also invade the flowers and cause damage to the base of floral parts so that they prematurely wilt and die, preventing fruit set. Thrips may transmit diseases from one plant to another.
Prevention/Control: Apply an insecticidal dust or spray, hang up sticky traps, use insect-proof netting.

Tomato Mite

These mites are many times smaller than the red spider mites that most gardeners are familiar with and can't be seen without the aid of a high-powered microscope. Under the microscope, spherical, clear eggs can be seen and the mite itself is shaped like a tiny maggot.
Symptoms: Heavily infested plants may develop bronze-coloured smooth stems and the leaves seem to be covered in a gold dust. Fruit can also be affected and will develop russet skins, sometimes with cracks around their circumference. The overall effect can be devastating. Tomato mites can turn a seemingly healthy plant into a drooping, stunted mess.
Prevention/Control: This is difficult. Apply a sulphur dust. If only one or two plants are infected, plant removal is the best control option to consider. Mites can be accidentally transferred from one plant to another by plant handlers or by people picking the fruit so be careful.

Tomato Stem Borer

The larvae, which grow up to 12 mm (½ in) long and are greyish green or pinkish.
Symptoms: Holes (usually 1 to 2 mm/$^1/_{10}$ in) wide on the stems. Larvae bore into the stems of tomato plants and travel downwards. They may

Tomato mites suck juice from tomato leaves and when present in large numbers can cause the leaves to curl back and die showing symptoms like leaf burning. The leaves also develop a speckled surface as shown here.

By the time gardeners notice the damage done by tomato stem borer larvae it is usually too late to save the plant because they have eaten the centre out of the stems, preventing the plant from functioning properly. This plant had holes in every stem and had collapsed completely.

bore along a leaf stalk to gain entry to the stem or straight into the stem if it is soft. Several grubs may attack a single plant and in severe cases the damage is so great that the plant wilts, collapses and dies, especially if it is stressed with a heavy crop.

Prevention/Control: Eggs from the moths can carry the infestation from one season to another if the crop residue is not hot composted or destroyed in autumn. These insects may also overwinter on evergreen black nightshade plants so remove black nightshade weeds. Control weeds, rotate crops, use insect-proof netting. Use an enclosed greenhouse.

Twenty-eight Spotted Ladybird

Organic gardeners usually try to attract various types of ladybirds into the garden to control pest insects such as aphids, but the twenty-eight spotted ladybird itself can become a pest. The larvae are about 6 mm (¼ in) long, greenish yellow with very thick black hairs poking up from the body. The adults are orange and have twenty-six to twenty-eight black spots on their domed, oval-shaped backs.

Symptoms: The larvae feed on tomato and potato plant leaves, eating the undersurface and leaving a network of leaf veins visible so that it is possible to see light through the damaged areas.

Prevention/Control: Collect by hand, apply an insecticidal dust or spray.

Vegetable Weevil/Elephant Beetle

These beetles have hard backs, are dome-shaped with a pronounced snout, about 9 mm ($1/3$ in) long, and often greyish brown. They may have soil attached to the body. The beetles move around at night and, if disturbed, will drop from the plant and 'play dead'.

Symptoms: Tomato plants are usually attacked by adults that chew small, often circular, holes at the edges of leaves, or partially chew leaves so that the veins are visible in the damaged area.

Prevention/Control: Collect by hand.

White Fly

White flies are very tiny (2 to 4 mm/$1/8$ in long) and triangular-shaped. They are usually found on the underside of the leaves and, if plants are brushed or disturbed, they will rise upwards in clouds from the leaves. The white fly adult can be seen with the naked eye, but the nymph stages are very hard to see without the aid of a small magnifying lens. Numbers can increase very quickly.

Symptoms: White flies suck the sap of tomato plants so they wilt and lose strength. The sugary plant extract which the flies deposit on the leaves often attracts ants or allows the growth of sooty mould.

Prevention/Control: These insects are very difficult to control, even with potent chemical sprays. Try insect-proof netting and sticky traps and sprays containing hot chilli extract. Gardeners of the future will probably be able to buy biological control agents (parasites) to use against this pest.

White Fringed Weevil

The larvae are curled, white to grey in colour, with brown heads. The adult is one of the elephant weevils (with a protruding snout from the head section), grey with a white band along the wing cover edge and can lay up to 1000 eggs during its short life cycle.

Symptoms: The larvae feed on the roots of tomato plants causing stunted growth. Adults may eat the foliage of the plant.

Prevention/Control: Collect by hand, grow green manure crops, let the soil lie fallow.

Wireworms (and False Wireworms)

Wireworms are soft and whitish with an orange head. The false wireworm larvae are cylindrical, yellow and reddish, or brown, and have defined solid segments. They are about 35 mm ($1\frac{1}{2}$ in) long, 4 to 5 mm ($\frac{1}{4}$ in) wide and slow moving.

Symptoms: They usually attack tuber crops such as potatoes, but the larvae sometimes attack young seedling tomato plant roots and the adults may bore into the stems below ground level. Attacks usually occur only when new ground has been prepared for tomato crops.

Prevention/Control: Let the soil lie fallow. Some gardeners bury cut potato tuber pieces or vegetable root crops in the soil to attract the wireworms away from the target crop.

An organic spray containing pyrethrum, garlic and hot chilli juice suitable for controlling most insects and pests.

5 Reaping the Rewards

Errol Stewart showing
just how tomatoes should
be consumed—fresh!

5.1 Harvesting and Storing

The time needed from seed sowing to harvest varies from 60 to 100 days depending on the climate and whether or not heating structures have been used.

Some home gardeners like to pick fruit when they are green then ripen them. If you want to do this, you must pick them at a *mature* green stage so the fruit will continue to ripen properly. If they are picked too early, they will not ripen evenly and be devoid of taste. You will have to find out for yourself, by trial and error, the correct mature green stage, as the fruits show no signs of maturity until they ripen and begin to change colour. For the best flavour, though, leave the tomatoes to ripen fully on the plant. Do not leave fruits on the plant after they are fully ripe as their flavour will decline and they may attract pests and diseases.

Harvesting

Once you are inundated with lovely home-grown tomatoes you will have to decide what to do with them because there might be too many to eat all at once. There are a range of options available. If you want to store them for a short time only, just store them as they are in a cool place (see below). Alternatively you can bottle them as a sauce, sun dry them or machine dry them for later use.

Storing

Tomatoes can be stored on a tray or shelves. Try to stop them from touching each other and use the ripest ones first. It is better to store them in a cool place out of direct sun. A special kind of plastic sheeting that absorbs ethylene (which ripens tomatoes) placed between the layers of packed tomatoes, will absorb excess carbon dioxide and thus delay the ripening of boxed fruits.

Storing Fresh

   Tomatoes placed in the refrigerator often show signs of chilling injury, so it is best not to store them this way. If stored below 11°C (52°F), they will collapse and start oozing water, and become very susceptible to skin and flesh rots. On the other hand they will not ripen properly in a temperature above 25°C (77°F). High temperatures interfere with the formation of the red pigment and the softening process is altered, so that they may go soft prematurely or the skin turn an insipid yellowy orange colour.

When tomatoes are in excess, try sun drying them.
1   Cut the tomatoes into thin slices and lay them on trays or racks.
2   Place a cover over them to keep away all insects. A thin mesh material is best as this allows the light to get in and air to move around the drying fruit. It is best to take the fruit inside or place it under shelter at night to keep it away from any dew or frost which would make it damp. Sun drying may take one or several days, depending on the heat of the sun.

Sun Drying

If you find sun drying too long and unreliable a process, there are several drying machines available capable of drying sliced fruit overnight. The

Machine Drying

machines are available from any shop selling electrical goods.

Tomato slices are dried to taste and the amount of drying depends on the end use.

☙ Chewy tomato slices can be for immediate use or for reconstituting.

☙ Slices as dry as chips can be eaten as chips or ground into powder or used in many other ways.

☙ Fruit leathers can be rolled up and stored, candied and used for sweets, placed in lunch boxes or reconstituted for cooking. Simply pulp the tomatoes, spread the mixture out as a sheet of liquid and then dry!

Any type of dried tomato slice can then be stored in pure or spiced olive oil in sealed bottles and will last for over a year. They can be dried or bottled with garlic or basil for extra flavour.

A RECIPE FOR DRYING

Cut the tomato into pieces about 5 to 8 mm (¼ in) thick. Use an electric drier and place the slices on the drying shelves. Sprinkle each piece of tomato with black pepper. Leave room for cloves of garlic to be placed between every other slice add powdered rock salt and a small amount of sugar, oregano and thyme. Thick wet slices may take a long time to dry.

5.2 Eating Tomatoes

One or two sliced unripe tomatoes added to any meal will actually enhance the tomato flavour of the ripe tomatoes used in the meal. There are many different ways of cooking tomatoes. From Italy comes paste and pizza sauces, from Greece sauces and preserves, from China wok-cooked foods, from America the hamburger and the Lebanese introduced salad oils. Australians have become a nation of tomato sauce lovers!

Tomato paste is now used in the preparation of inumerable dishes, is contained in concentrated tomato juice, and is an ingredient in the well known 'Bloody Mary' cocktail. Thousands of tomatoes are consumed every year in various types of tomato sandwiches. What would an Aussie barbeque be like without the sausages and tomato sauce; the steak and onions and tomato; and the hamburger, tomato and salad? Tomatoes are added to stews, soups, sauces, seafood dishes, curries and cakes.

With modern cooking and food preparation equipment, you can freeze-dry tomatoes or sun dry tomatoes. You can juice whole tomatoes in a juice extractor, deep freeze tomatoes or make chip-like flakes or powder from dried tomatoes to be used in cooking.

5.3 Recipes

There must be thousands of different ways to eat tomatoes. Following is a small collection of recipes and snacks given by friends, relatives, aquaintances, cousins, associates, listeners to Melbourne's 3CR radio gardening show and gardeners kind enough to offer their secret cooking and preserving ideas for this book.

Green tomatoes can be picked at any time to make pickles.

At the end of the season as tomato plants start to die, whole plants can be pulled up and hung on a wall or in a shed to allow the remaining green fruits to ripen.

To extend the ripening period of tomato plants, plastic sheeting can be placed over them (making sure it does not touch the foliage).

Sun drying of tomatoes can easily be done in warm-climate areas, but you may need to protect the drying fruits from flies and wasps using fine mesh.

Health Tidbits

YELLOW FRUIT ARE LOW IN ACID MYTH

Many people suffering from arthritis believe that food from the Solonaceae family (to which tomatoes belong) will aggravate the disease. Some think that yellow tomatoes are lower in acid and therefore safer to eat but this is a myth. Although some yellow tomatoes are lower in acid than some red ones, it does not follow that all yellow tomatoes are low in acid. The low-acid characteristic is tied to the kind of tomato not its colour. Tomato fruit pulp varies in acidity from about pH 4.2 to pH 4.5.

CANCER CURE

A report in the *Herald Sun* (7 Dec 1995) mentions research done by Dr Edward Giovannucci at Harvard University. His research provides statistical evidence connecting the eating of tomatoes and the incidence of prostate cancer. Male persons eating tomatoes regularly have far less chance of contracting prostate cancer. A survey of 47,000 men over a nine-year period showed that those persons eating tomato products in various forms such as sauce, juice, cooked in pizzas or as spaghetti sauce, or raw significantly reduced the risk of cancer of the prostate.

Snacks

Ruth's Seafood Frolic

A sauce for fresh uncooked oysters.

Ruth Cosgrove, a young food-consuming expert, passes this recipe on to those who like the good life.

Collect tomato paste and fresh cream. Mix these ingredients in a 50:50 ratio. Add chopped fresh basil to taste. Eat this with natural oysters and enjoy!

Errol's Passion

Fresh fruit off the vine.

Errol Stewart has a passionate relationship with tomato fruits. He just cannot walk past a dish, bowl, display or growing plant with nice red juicy tomatoes without picking some to eat raw. In fact, he recommends tomato lovers always to eat them fresh.

Tomatoes cut and placed on a fruit drying tray. The small cherry tomatoes, although seemingly full of seed, had the best taste after drying.

The tomato slices have reduced in size after being dried but, oh, the taste sensation!

'There is no need to cook, bake, jam, sauce or fry tomatoes,' he says. 'They taste as good as, if not better than, apples' and he consumes many kilos a week when tomatoes are in season. If you invite Errol to your house, hide the tomatoes!

Jack's Tomato Breakfast Feast

This is not a recipe for the diet conscious, but it tastes superb. It is a good snack for that wake-me-up-in-the-morning feeling.

Buy or bake some fresh bread and cut it into very thick slices of about 1 to 2 cm (1 in). Put these on a plate and pour and spread cream evenly over the bread about ½ cm (¼ in) thick. Allow a few minutes for the cream to soak all the way through the bread then cut a large tasty tomato into slices about 1 cm (½ in) thick and place these on the bread. Sprinkle the tomato slices with a little salt and pepper to taste. Sit down and have a good snack.

Wealth-deprived Person's Tomato Meal

This is an age-old recipe passed down by Europeans—it may have originated in Greece or Italy.

Use large slices of bread, preferably fresh but, for cheapness, old or stale bread can be used. The slices can be toasted or untoasted according to taste. The bread is spread with a liberal layer of pure olive oil. Let the oil soak through the bread then place tomato slices on it. A sprinkle of mixed dried herbs or fresh herbs if available (usually including basil) is put on the tomato slices and it is ready to eat.

Allen's Bread Slice

One of the author's experiments!

Use thick slices of herbal or multi-grained bread, spread a little butter on the bread then take a wedge of Brie cheese and spread this over the surface. Put some hot salami on the cheese and top with slices of a tasty tomato. Add a light sprinkle, of salt and pepper. A delicious tasty dish and 'a meal in a bite'!

Jack's tomato breakfast feast (bread, cream, salt and pepper).

Tomato and Cheese Paste

A recipe from Dorothy Manning that has been passed down through the family from her grandmother.

This spread is delicious on cheese biscuits, as a sandwich filling or placed on bread and then toasted under a grill. This recipe makes only one jar and Dorothy says it is so tasty it will not last long, so maybe you will have to double the amount.

750 g (1½ lb) tomatoes   **salt, pepper and mustard to taste**
500 g (1 lb) cheese, finely grated

Peel the tomatoes, chop finely and boil well. Add the cheese, salt, pepper and mustard to taste. Simmer until the cheese has completely melted. When the mix has cooled, place it in a jar and store in the refrigerator.

Fruity Baked Tomatoes

6 medium-sized tomatoes   **2 tbsp currants**
1 cup cooked rice   **1 clove garlic, crushed**
1 tbsp onion, chopped   **salt and pepper**

Remove the top from the stem end of the tomatoes, scoop out the flesh and mix it with the the rice, onion, currants, garlic, salt and pepper. Spoon the mixture into the hollowed-out tomatoes. Simmer in a casserole dish with half to one cup of water.

Fit the lid and bake for 20 to 30 minutes in a medium oven which has been pre-heated.

Phyllis's Breadline Tomato and Onion Pie

Serve this with roast lamb or beef.

tomatoes, sliced   **stale bread**
onions, finely sliced   **butter**
seasoning

Grease an enamel or pyrex plate or dish and cover the base of the dish with tomatoes. Place onions over the tomato slices, season, then sprinkle with dry breadcrumbs. Repeat this layering sequence again and again if needed. Dot with small lumps of butter.

Bake in a moderate oven for approximately 60 minutes.

Tomatoes Pennsylvania

An old recipe for a sauce to use on grilled meat, entrees or toast from Elizabeth Jenkins.

1 kg (2 lb) tasty tomatoes   **margarine for frying (or butter)**
plain flour   **brown sugar**
pepper and salt to taste   **cream**

Trim the stem ends of the tomatoes to remove the stems and take a thin slice off the basal end. Cut the tomatoes into very thick slices and roll these in flour, adding pepper and salt. Fry the slices in a little margarine (or butter) on one side and then the other to produce a browning on both surfaces. Sprinkle one side with brown sugar and let it melt into the tomato. Pour cream on top of the slices and serve.

2 tomatoes
1 onion
1 tbsp sugar
½ tsp bicarbonate of soda
2 tsp cornflour
1 to 2 cups water

Cut the tomatoes and onion into small pieces and place in a bowl and cook in the microwave for 10 to 20 minutes. Push the cooked mix through a sieve and add sugar and bicarbonate of soda to the liquid. Mix the cornflour with water and stir it in with the other ingredients. Cook the mix in the microwave until it boils. It is now ready to serve.

½ cup uncooked rice
500 g (1 lb) minced steak
salt and pepper
1 small onion, chopped
½ cup celery, chopped
3 tbsp butter
2 to 3 cups tomato puree

Wash and drain the rice and put in a bowl. Add the seasoned mince steak and salt and pepper to taste. Mix well and shape the mix into balls, pressing firmly. Place the meat balls in a casserole dish.

Sauté the onion and celery in butter for 5 minutes, add the tomato puree, stir well then pour this over the meat balls.

Bake in a moderate oven for 90 minutes, removing the lid for the last 30 minutes — then eat!

**Sauces, Relishes,
Chutneys and
Pickles**

Bottled Tomatoes

Mary Michaux has been using this recipe for over 50 years.

2 kg (4 lb) onions
2 kg (4 lb) green tomatoes
4 handfuls salt
2 L (2 quarts) vinegar
1 cup plain flour
2 cups sugar
2 tbsp mustard
2 tbsp turmeric

Cut the onions and tomatoes into small pieces, add the salt and allow this mix to stand overnight. The next day, boil the onions and tomatoes in their own juice for 10 minutes then strain. Add the vinegar and boil for 10 minutes. Add the dry ingredients then boil for another 10 minutes. Bottle the mixture when it has cooled but is still warm.

Tomato Sauce

There are probably thousands of tomato sauce recipes throughout the world. This one has been passed down by Vera Storer's grandmother. Vera is an octogenarian who has been making this brew every year of her married life and has never had one bottle ferment.

30 g (1 oz) pimento
30 g (1 oz) cloves
5½ kg (12 lb) tomatoes, peeled and
   chopped
750 g (1½ lb) onions, peeled and
   chopped
1 kg (2 lb) cooking apples
30 g (1 oz) garlic
1 kg (2½ lb) sugar
120 g (4 oz) salt
30 g (1 oz) ground ginger
1 L (1 quart) vinegar

Place the pimento and cloves in cloth bags. Boil all the other ingredients, except the vinegar, with a little water for 1 hour. Then add the vinegar and boil for a further 2 hours. Leave the mix to cool and then strain it. Bottle the ingredients and seal the containers with paraffin wax.

Tomato Relish

3 kg (6 lb) ripe tomatoes, skins removed
1 kg (2 lb) onions
1 small handful salt
1 kg (2 lb) sugar
1 tsp cayenne pepper
3 tsp mustard
2 tsp curry powder
¼ L (½ pint) brown vinegar

Cut the tomatoes and onions. Place these in separate bowls and use half the salt on each; allow to stand overnight. The next day, strain them and place them in a pot with the remaining ingredients except for the mustard, curry powder and vinegar. Cook for 5 minutes only then remove from the heat. Add the mustard and curry powder which has been prepared by mixing to a paste with a little vinegar. Pour over enough of the vinegar just to cover the mixture then boil for 1 hour. Bottle while still hot.

French Chutney

A recipe obtained from a free booklet issued by plant nurseries and received from Pat Taylor. Pat has been using this recipe since 1986 and it has become a favourite of the family. Maybe it's one that you should try for your family. This recipe makes about 1½ L (2½ pints) of chutney.

1 kg (2 lb) tomatoes
3 large onions, peeled and chopped
3 small Granny Smith cooking apples
¼ cup currants
½ cup sultanas
5 cups brown vinegar
½ tsp curry powder
1 tbsp salt
1 tsp whole cloves
750 g (1½ lb) sugar

Dip the tomatoes in hot then cold water then remove the skins. Chop them up into chunky bits. Place all of the ingredients in a large pan, heat and stir until the sugar has dissolved. Simmer without the lid on the pan for about 2½ hours or until the chutney thickens.

Prepare hot sterilised jars, bottle the chutney and seal the jars.

Fruit Chutney

A recipe from John Small.

1 kg (2 lb) jam melon (it looks like a water melon but has yellow flesh)
1 kg (2 lb) apples
250 g (½ lb) green tomatoes
250 g (½ lb) onions
500 g (1 lb) sugar
125 g (¼ lb) preserved ginger
2 small tsp cloves
2 small tsp pimento, whole
1 tsp salt
1 small tsp mustard seed
½ L (1 pint) vinegar

Peel, seed and cut the melon into small blocks. Boil it in a little water until three-parts cooked (blocks still solid but softened) then drain the mix. Add all the other ingredients with the cloves and pimento tied in a spice bag. Simmer all ingredients in the vinegar until a good colour and consistency is reached (it usually takes about 2 hours). Bottle the chutney when cold.

For those living in the far north. This mix produces about 5 kg (10 lb) of chutney.

Queensland Fruit Chutney

2 kg (4 lb) of apples
1 kg (2 lb) pears
1½ kg (3 lb) tomatoes
1 level tsp mace
250 g (½ lb) sultanas
250 g (½ lb) seedless raisins
2 kg (4 lb) sugar

2 L (2 quarts) vinegar
1 level tsp cayenne pepper
1 tsp cloves
1 tsp peppercorns
2 tbsp salt
1 tsp ground ginger

Peel the apples and pears, core them and cut into small pieces. Skin the tomatoes and add to the apple and pear pieces. Add the remaining ingredients and some water and simmer the mix for 2 hours. Bottle while hot and seal when cold.

This recipe is for those gardeners who have too many tomatoes or have late-picked tomatoes that are slow to ripen.

Jack Rae's Green Tomato Pickles

3 kg (6 lb) green tomatoes, sliced
2 tbsp salt
750 g (1½ lb) brown onions, sliced
600 g (1¼ lb) sugar
just over 1 L (1 quart) good brown
   vinegar

1 dessertspoon curry powder
2 tbsp plain flour
45 g (1½ oz) of turmeric (to add
   colour)

Place the sliced tomatoes in cooking pan and sprinkle the salt over them. Tilt the pan on its side and allow to stand overnight. The next day, drain the liquid, add the onions, sugar and vinegar and cook until the fruit is soft. Make sure not to over-cook, as the onions need to be firm and not mushy. Mix the curry powder, flour and turmeric with some vinegar to a paste. Add the paste to the fruit while the contents of the pan are 'off the boil'. Gradually bring back to boiling point and stir constantly until the pickles thicken. Bottle when cool.

3 kg (6 lb) green tomatoes
2 kg (4 lb) onions
handful salt
vinegar, enough to cover the
   chopped tomatoes and onions

sugar to taste
2 whole cloves
1 tsp cayenne pepper
flour, mustard and turmeric
   according to taste

Rosie's Green Tomato Pickles

Chop the tomatoes and onions, sprinkle with salt and leave to stand overnight. The next morning, drain the liquid off, cover the tomatoes with vinegar and add the sugar. Place two whole cloves in a muslin bag and add this with the cayenne pepper to the tomatoes and onions. Boil for 20 minutes. Mix the flour, mustard and turmeric into a paste with some vinegar. Add this to the tomatoes and onions and boil the mix for another 15 minutes. Remove the pan from the heat. Bottle into sterilised jars.

Green Tomato and Cucumber Pickles

2¼ kg (5 lb) green tomatoes
2¼ kg (5 lb) cucumbers
2¼ kg (5 lb) onions
1 dessertspoon salt
vinegar, enough to cover chopped
    tomatoes, cucumbers and
    onions

1 tsp turmeric
2 tbsp mustard
1 small tsp pepper
3 cups sugar
1 cup flour

Cut up the tomatoes, cucumbers and onions and arrange in sliced layers, with salt between each layer, in a small dish. Leave overnight. The next morning, drain off the juice, cover with vinegar and boil until soft, adding sugar to taste. Thicken the mix with flour and spices. Bottle when cold.

Jams

Red or Green Tomato Jam

1 kg (2 lb) tomatoes
1 kg (2 lb) sugar

4 tbsp lemon juice
½ tsp ginger (optional)

Cut the tomatoes into quarters and cover them with sugar. Allow the mix to stand overnight. Simmer gently, stirring well, until all sugar has dissolved, then continue simmering until tomatoes are soft. Add the lemon juice and ginger if needed and then boil rapidly until the mixture becomes very thick. Pour into sterilised jars and seal when cool.

Tomato and Ginger Jam

3 kg (6½ lb) ripe tomatoes
3 medium-sized lemons
⅓ cup preserved ginger pieces in
    syrup
7 cups sugar

Peel the tomatoes, chop them into pieces and put aside. Peel the lemons thinly so as not to remove too much pith. Cut the peel of two lemons into match-thin strips and put aside. Squeeze and strain the juice from all the lemons. Chop the ginger into small pieces. Put all the ingredients into a saucepan and bring to the boil. Stir rapidly until all the sugar has dissolved. Boil quickly until setting point is reached. Pour into sterilised jars and seal.

Marge's Pineapple and Tomato Jam

Marge Hancock remembers all the old ways and some of the old recipes that her mother used. This is a special one on how to make tomato and pineapple jam.

Use 7 kg (15 lb) of tomatoes and plunge them into boiling water so that the skins come off easily. Take six large pineapples, peel and cut them into small pieces. Skin the tomatoes and mix them with the pineapple. Stew the mix gently until the pineapple pieces become soft, add 340 g (¾ lb) of sugar for each half-kilo (pound) of the original mixture and boil until thick enough to bottle.

800 g (1¾ lb) quinces

1 kg (2 lb) ripe tomatoes

2½ cups water

2 kg (4½ lb) sugar

Peel, core and slice the quinces. Pour boiling water over the tomatoes and remove their skins. Simmer the fruits in the water for 1½ hours. Add the sugar and boil rapidly until setting point is reached. Pour into sterilised jars and allow to set.

George Edson offers this solution to an oversupply of tomato fruits.

- ✆ Using a deep bowl to hold the fruit, place it in a microwave oven and cook for a while so that the fruit turns to pulp. This pulp can be mixed with vinegar, oil or sugar and then stored in sterilised containers in the deep freeze.
- ✆ Tomato fruit can also be juiced through a vitamiser and the juice stored for a few days in the refrigerator or treated in the same way as pulp.

500 g (1 lb) tomatoes

½ tsp salt

½ cup water

1 dessertspoon sugar

Worcestershire sauce

lemon juice

Skin and chop the tomatoes. Put them in a saucepan with the salt, water and sugar. Cover and simmer until the mix is soft and pulpy. Pour and rub the mix through a coarse strainer or blend with a blender. Refrigerate. Add Worcestershire sauce and lemon juice to taste and serve in a small glass. The juice will keep for three to four days.

SUNBURN RELIEF

I remember when I was young (with blue eyes and fair skin) often being sunburnt. One of the most successful remedies for immediate sunburn relief was to place tomato juice from a sliced tomato (or cow's milk) onto the burnt area when it became painful. Cool tomato juice felt great and seemed to work well to reduce the pain. (It is better, however, to cover up and avoid sunburn and the almost inevitable skin cancer.)

Cultivars Old and New

THE GOOD OLD DAYS

Before the days of the large international seed companies distributing seed everywhere, home gardeners saved their own seeds and shared the seed among friends. In those days they did not choose to grow tomatoes for their skin hardiness, or eveness of maturity, but judged the quality of a tomato mainly by taste and the use it was to be put to.

Three generations of tomato growers (Ahmed Seih and his father and son) and a tomato fruit grown from seed that has been saved and passed on by family members.

BREEDING

Over the years from natural variation within seedling plants, gardeners, research workers and seed firms all over the world have gradually selected tomatoes for various attributes: early, mid- and late-season ripening, dwarf, tall and creeping plant forms and so on. Breeders have produced tomato plants which are better adapted to growing in a range of climates and situations, including cool and warm climates, pots, glasshouses and open fields. Tomatoes were also bred for all kinds of culinary uses, e.g. pasta tomatoes, salad tomatoes and tomatoes for bottling, chutney, drying, jam making, juicing, sauces, soups, stewing and stuffing.

Recently plant breeders have mapped the tomato plant's genetic code with its twelve chromosomes and have found most of the genes responsible for various traits such as skin colour (clear skin, red, orange, white, green or black), leaf shape, plant size, fruit shape, virus resistance, ripening time, and many more.

THE TASTELESS TOMATO TAKEOVER

Tomato breeders who have concentrated on the qualities suitable for producing fruits for canning, though, have inadvertently got rid of the

Mechanical harvesting of tomato fruits in Victoria, Australia, enabling thousands of tomatoes to be picked, sorted and packed daily.

Mechanical harvesting rips the whole plant from the ground. This photo shows the trash left behind after the harvester has passed.

true taste of the tomato. In America during the 1980s, tomatoes grown for canning often had to have vitamins and minerals added during the canning process to provide taste! The discovery of a method of ripening tomatoes using ethylene gas enabled growers to pick the tomatoes while they were hard and green, and thus reduce bruising. Simultaneously, most of the popular varieties were discontinued because they were too soft, bruised easily, were too juicy, would not store well, were susceptible to pests or diseases, or did not produce a large even crop. Plants were rejected because they were the wrong size for mechanical harvesting, or the fruit was too large or too small for the machines used in the canning process.

Tomatoes developed for canning became the most common cultivars in shops because fruit that was in oversupply to the canneries flooded the markets. These secondgrade or surplus tomatoes sold very cheaply, making it hard for shopkeepers to sell other selected varieties that had cost more to produce.

SEED SAVERS' NETWORKS

Media coverage about environmental issues, today's awareness of the destruction of genetic resource materials, the taking over of seed companies (in the United States) by multi-nationals, the passing of laws (in some countries) to prevent persons selling old-variety tomato seeds and talk of biogenetic breeding programs all prompted the formation of seed savers' networks.

Seed savers' networks rely on home gardeners to save their own seed and then send some of it to the seed savers' network headquarters. All seed sources and a description of the different varieties available are listed in a periodical sent to all members annually by the seed savers' networks so that the seed from one home gardener can be used by many. Some of these seeds have been passed on from family members to other family members for generations and have never been sold commercially.

There are a number of seed savers' networks throughout the world including China. The network exchange in the United States has over 4000 registered tomato seed varieties with names such as 'Abe Lincoln', 'Ace', 'Black Hawk', 'Craw Put', 'Dansk Export', 'Egyptian Tomb', 'Kusky's Big Blocky Italian', 'Mayan Indian', 'Punjab Chuhara', 'Purple Price', 'Red Alert', 'Russian Apple Tree', 'Softball Grandma Nelly Campbell', 'Whippersnapper', 'Yellow Jumbo Heirloom' — and hundreds more. As far as I know none of these has ever been grown in Australia. The Seed Savers' Network of Byron Bay, Australia, has about 200 varieties listed. Tomatoes listed in the Australian Heritage Seed Curators' network catalogue lists nine pages of heritage tomatoes that are no longer available in Australia and Digger's Seed Company, Dromana, have imported some heritage seeds from America which are now available to home gardeners.

MANIPULATING GENES

Plant breeders using today's knowledge and techniques can transfer genes from one plant species into another unrelated species; even animal genes can now be inserted into plant material. This enables breeders to virtually program or build a plant with all the characteristics they need, although most of the plants produced will probably not grow true to type from seed. Many people are concerned that biogenetic material may introduce a new disease into a plant system that will be almost impossible to control.

The first genetically engineered tomato ('Flava Sava') was released in the United States during the summer of 1994. Scientists predict that by 1998 the commercial production of a tomato containing the gene for the production of the toxin associated with *Bacillus thuringiensis* (the material toxic to many leaf eating caterpillars) will have started. Tomatoes with an inserted gene to 'turn off' the rotting of fruit once it is ripe have already been bred. There is less fruit spoilage and increased production at harvest time with these genetically altered tomatoes. The pulp provides a thicker paste, and the amount of energy needed for processing is said to be significantly reduced. These tomatoes were on sale in shops in the United Kingdom during August of 1996 and store managers reported a positive consumer acceptance with increased sales.

In Australia researchers have discovered several *Solanum* species used by indigenous people and these are now being collected or grown and sold as 'bush tucker' food. The group of plants include *S. chippendalei* (the bush tomato), *S. centrale* (bush raisin) and *S. ellipticum* (the desert raisin). Gardeners of the future may be able to buy these plants for the home garden or use the plants as rootstocks for the common tomato enabling the plants to survive for many seasons.

Future tomato varieties may be biogenetically engineered to repel pests, be totally disease resistant, or tolerant of extreme saline or acid soils, for example. Engineered plants may even grow two types of crops such as a potato and tomato to achieve maximum production and reduce reliance upon insecticides and fungicides that are poisoning and polluting the environment.

Chart 1: Cultivar/Variety Selection

There have been thousands of tomato varieties bred and selected over hundreds of years but many are no longer available to home gardeners even through the seed savers' networks and specialist growers and seed firms.

William Watson, in his comprehensive six-volume work *The Gardener's Assistant* (1936), mentions that there were about 200 tomato varieties available in England at that time. Many of those old English varieties, such as 'Ailsa Craig', have been imported into Australia.

The following selection includes new varieties and old heritage varieties and many of the ever popular old tomato types still grown today.

Big Red

Apollo Improved

Amish Paste

Chart 1: Cultivar/Variety Selection

| Cultivar/ Variety | Description | | Season (early, mid, late) | Special Uses | Taste | | Comments |
	Fruit	Plant			Digger's Seeds Ranking	Author & Home Gardeners	
Ailsa Craig	Clusters of medium-sized tomatoes, round as billiard balls, tough skinned and rarely cracking.	Bush forming and suitable for cool climates and glasshouses.		Drying, tomato sauce.		Good	Old-English favourite from yesteryear. Popular variety in William Watson's publication of 1936.
Amish Paste	Red, very large and heart-shaped. Thick flesh and few seeds.			Suitable for stewing, bottling, stuffing or for paste.	11	Great	An ancient variety preserved by the Amish community. Heirloom variety.
Apollo Improved	Medium-sized.	A reliable producer. Sets fruit even when cool nights are experienced. A strong-growing plant needing stakes or a growing frame.	Early		10	Great	A hybrid tomato resistant to verticillium. Very popular with home gardeners. Begins cropping about 8 weeks from planting and continues for an extended period.
Arcadia	Medium to small. Can be left on bush to ripen. They are picked with the calyx attached to make an attractive presentation.						A bush tomato developed by commercial growers and the Victorian Dept of Agriculture. This tomato is bringing taste back into the kitchen and is very popular.
Azoychka	Large, flattened and yellow.	A staking tomato.				Excellent	Unusual. Coloured fruits do not look appetising.
Beefmaster	One of the largest. Solid with few seeds.	Tall growing with medium-sized crops.		Sandwich making, baking and stewing.			F_1 hybrid.

Chart 1 (continued)

Variety	Fruit	Plant	Use	Taste	Notes
Beefsteak	Named for its solid flesh. Slightly ribbed with few seeds and can grow very large (2 kg/4 lb).	Vigorous and will need staking, a trellis or other support.	Sliced fresh fruit, salads.	Sweet	Does not tolerate temperatures above 32°C (90°F). Side shoots can be pinched off to obtain larger tomatoes.
Bellstar	Large, plum-like and can weigh 170 g (6 oz) or more.	Bush form.	Reputedly developed for making pastes and juices. Also suitable for salads.		
Best of All	Good size. Deep scarlet.	Produces heavy bunches of fruit at short intervals all over the plant.			One of the favourites recorded by William Watson (1936).
Big Red	Large (up to ½ kg/1 lb) with not many seeds.	Staking is needed.		Good	One of the most popular with home gardeners.
Big Yellow	Low acid. Turn from green to yellow.	Tall growing.			Pruning is usually recommended.
Black Beefsteak	Black areas at the top and blackish purple inside.	Tall growing. 'Beefsteak' characteristics.		Excellent	Colour can be off-putting.
Black Russian	Dark blackish brown or purple on the shoulders or over the entire surface. Darkened flesh with creamy texture. Like 'Beefsteak'.	Vigorous and needs staking.		Taste diminishes when overripe	The appearance can be off-putting, but once you taste it you will go on growing it forever. Probably many forms available in home-garden collections.
Bon Gusto	Huge, red and slightly ribbed.	Medium cropper with medium bush form.	Sandwiches		Tasting the fruit will make gardeners want to grow this variety.

Chart I (continued)

Cultivar/ Variety	Description		Season (early, mid, late)	Special Uses	Taste		Comments
	Fruit	Plant			Digger's Seeds Ranking	Author & Home Gardeners	
Bonny Best	Large, bright (almost iridescent), pinky red fruit, which grow in small clusters.	Tall growing. Vigorous grower and needs staking.	Mid				An old market-garden selection, once common in NSW.
Brandy Wine	Medium-sized. Pinky purple or deep red.	Tall with potato-type leaves. Suitable for staking.		Slices well and often used in salads.			This plant can be traced back to the late 1800s, when it was selected and grown by the Amish community in Pennsylvania.
Break O'Day	Medium to large. Orangy red, smooth, round and firm. Resistant to tomato wilt and will grow in most climates.	Tall with sparse foliage.	Early	Canning, stewing.			Bred by the United States Dept. of Agriculture. Resistant to wilt and will grow in most climates. The fruit skins are soft and therefore not suitable for packing.
Broad Ripple Yellow Currant	Tiny—the size of a cherry tomato. Bright yellow and hangs in clusters from the plant.	A creeping, vigorous, twining plant that needs support by staking or trellis.		Bite size for salads and plate decoration.	4	Excellent	Seedlings could probably be used as rootstocks for grafting other tomato plants onto.
Burbank	Bright red fruit of an even size, with thin skin that peels easily.	A bush tomato.		Suitable for all uses. Salads, sauce, bottling, juice.			Luther Burbank was the first American nurseryman to use natural selection of forced crosses to produce superior plants. His tomato was probably vastly superior to all others available at the time. It will store well, is resistant to wilt and will grow in cool areas.

Colossal Yellow

Peruvian Currant

Bon Gusto

Gardener's Delight

Black Russian

Dwarf Wax

Chart 1 (continued)

Cultivar/ Variety	Description		Season (early, mid, late)	Special Uses	Taste		Comments
	Fruit	Plant			Digger's Seeds Ranking	Author & Home Gardeners	
Burnley Bounty	Juicy, medium-sized and round. Develop a glorious taste if left on the vine to ripen.	Vigorous.	Early	Bottling, sauce, fresh.			Bred by Helgi Nirk, at the Victorian Dept of Agriculture, this tall-growing plant is a cross between 'Grosse Lisse' and the wild Peruvian tomato *L. peruvianum*. Resists fusarium wilt, is cold tolerant and will grow in most soil types.
Burnley Gem	Medium-sized, slightly ribbed and rounded.	Dwarf bush. Has naturally rolled leaves and produces crops over a long period. OK for pots.		Bottling, sauce, fresh.			Bred at the Victorian Dept of Agriculture. Generally suitable for growing north of the Great Dividing Range. Is resistant to fusarium wilt and is a heavy cropper that will do well in cool areas.
Burnley Surecrop	As the name suggests, an assured crop of medium-sized, juicy, round fruit (similar to 'Grosse Lisse').	Tall growing. Will need staking or support.					Resistant to verticillium wilt and can be planted in disease-ridden beds.
Burwood Prize also called Burwood Wonder	Medium to large. Plenty of juice and flavour.	Vigorous and hardy. A light bearer.		Juicing, fresh.			What these plants lack in quantity, they make up for in flavour.
Chalk's Early Jewel	Very large, scarlet-red fruit that are solid and meaty.	A bush-type plant.		Sauce, paste, drying.		Sweet	The plant has lots of foliage so is not prone to sun scald. Is also resistant to tomato blight. Recommended.

Chart 1 (continued)

Variety	Fruit	Plant	Use	Season/climate	No.	Taste	Notes
Cherry Cocktail (3 tomatoes, red, orange and yellow, in one pot)	Large clusters of cherry-sized fruits.	Vigorous. Will need staking or support.	Salad—different colours.		9	Sweet	Great for self-professed hopeless gardeners, as they will grow anywhere. Can be picked from the vine as they mature.
Chinese Orange	Medium-sized, round and fleshy. Not a lot of juice. The skin turns a brilliant orange colour at maturity.	Vigorous, but not very tolerant of wet conditions.	Chinese farmers grow this fruit specifically for drying.	Suitable for dry, hot, inland areas			A selection brought back from China by the author, its origins are Turpan, in the centre of the Gobi desert, one of the driest hottest places on earth. Not available from seed companies or seed savers' networks.
College Challenger	Prolific crops of medium to large meaty tomatoes.	A vigorous plant that needs support. Grows well in hot and cool areas.		Mid to late			Bred at Hawkesbury Agricultural College, NSW. A cross between 'Grosse Lisse' and 'Tatura Dwarf Giobe'.
Colossal Yellow	Large, juicy and a beautiful pale yellow colour. 'Beefsteak'-like.	Tall, vigorous and heavy bearing. Survives hot weather well.	Useful for slicing and for using in salads, providing an unusual colour to the dinner plate.		22	Not startling	
Costoluto Genovese	Flattened, unusual shape and strongly ribbed.		Makes wonderful sauce. Stuffing.			Great taste	Similar to a Costoluto cultivar brought from Italy by Don Burke. An old Italian cultivar. Several cultivars originate from the Costoluto area in Italy. Included in a mixed seed pack with other paste tomatoes sold by Digger's Seeds.

Chart I (continued)

Cultivar/Variety	Description — Fruit	Description — Plant	Season (early, mid, late)	Special Uses	Taste — Digger's Seeds Ranking	Taste — Author & Home Gardeners	Comments
Daydream	Large, red and rounded, but slightly flat.	Staking is required. Will do well in dry areas.					Susceptible to soil-borne tomato diseases, so grow in above-ground containers or pots or graft it onto a disease-resistant stock plant.
Dixie Golden Giant	A good crop. Large, lemony yellow with few seeds. 'Beefsteak' type. (This means solid flesh with very few seeds.)					Sweet	
Duke	Large 'Oxheart'-like.	Bush-like growth habit.	Early			Mild	Resistant to root rotting fungi that cause verticillium and fusarium wilt, so could be used as rootstocks.
Dwarf Wax	Large and yellow. When ripe, a dark marking appears on the shoulder.					Good	
Earliest of All	Bright red with a wonderful juicy texture.	Great cropper. Is vigorous and bush forming and will produce crops in cool areas.	Early	Fresh, sauces.		Good	
Egg Quick Pick	Egg-shaped with very little seed, so mostly flesh. Low in acid.	A spreading bush habit. Grows very quickly.		Superb for cooking and drying.			A popular Yates variety.
First Prize	Rounded, medium-sized and solid.	Vigorous. Can be grown in pots.	Early			Good	A hybrid that is resistant to verticillium and fusarium wilts.

112

Chart I (continued)

113

Four-colour Cherry Mixed	Small, round, different coloured fruits.	Some gardeners like to plant all the cultivars in a circle to make picking and management easier. It also provides wind protection and helps retain heat.	Salads, fresh, drying. A Digger's Seeds recommendation for those who want tasty tomatoes and bright colours in their salads.	Early		Excellent	Made up from Pink Cherry, Broad Ripple Yellow Currant, Red Cherry, Scotland Yellow, Orange Sundrop.
Gardeners' Delight	Cherry type.	Indeterminate (branches keep growing) growth habit. Can be staked.	Salads, fresh, drying.		8	Rich	
Gold Dust	Round and orange.	Determinate (growth ceases at top of shoots when plant flowers) growth. Cold tolerant.				Good	
Golden Delight	Medium-sized, flattened and globe shaped. Orangy yellow skin.						
Golden Sunrise	Small, round and golden. Low in acid.	Prodigious crops. Vigorous vine. Staking or support needed.	Low acid meals.				
Golden Tomato Gourmet Filler	Medium-sized, golden yellow with open cavities.	A vigorous vine.	The hollow cavities make it good for stuffing.				Flavour enhanced by cooking/stuffing.
Graf Zeppelin	Medium-sized and red.	Vigorous.				Great	
Green and Yellow Top Tasting			Salads			Tasty	A seed mix. Made up from Broad Ripple Yellow Currant, Golden Sunrise, Green Zebra.

Chart I (continued)

Cultivar/ Variety	Description		Season (early, mid, late)	Special Uses	Taste		Comments
	Fruit	Plant			Digger's Seeds Ranking	Author & Home Gardeners	
Greenwich	Medium-sized with greenish yellow skin and flesh. The sliced flesh has a beautiful symmetrical pattern, offset by the unusual colour.					Excellent	Fruit have a long storage potential.
Green Zebra	Small to medium-sized. Ripens to a greenish colour with beautiful green stripes, the background skin providing yellow flecks.				16	Excellent	Digger's Seeds guarantee 15 kg (33 lb) from this plant. Don't wait for them to turn red. They are green when ripe.
Grosse Lisse	Clusters of medium-sized fruit.	Vigorous, needs support, crops well.		The lot.	15	Wonderful	A perennial favourite of Australian home gardeners. Has topped the list of several tomato tasting competitions.
Harbinger	Medium-sized with thin skins.	Needs a stake or trellis.					One of the oldest tomatoes known, it continues to be popular for both open growing and glasshouse production.
Hardy Tom	Small (bite-sized) with tough skin.	Spreading vigorous vine. Produces masses of fruit for many months (if sheltered).					Resists fruit fly attack. Cold tolerant.
Italian Paste Mixed		Most plants small to dwarf in size and easily grown.		Suitable for making pastas and pizza sauce.			An 'Italian' seed mix from Digger's Seeds. Made up from Ballerina, Marzano Lampadina, Napoli, San Marzano.

Scotland Yellow

Tiny Tim

Roma

Sweet 100

Red Peach

Stuffing Tomato

Chart I (continued)

Cultivar/Variety	Description		Season (early, mid, late)	Special Uses	Taste		Comments
	Fruit	Plant			Digger's Seeds Ranking	Author & Home Gardeners	
Italian Plum	Flattened, ribbed and deep reddish purple. The flesh is thick and meaty.	A vigorous plant.		Excellent for pasta, sauce and drying.			
Jubilee	Large (up to 10 cm/4 in) in diameter. Golden yellow, fleshy with thick walls. Low in acid.	Tall growing and will grow in a large range of climatic conditions. May need staking or a support.					A colour treat for the garden.
Kelstar	Attractive, medium-sized.	Very vigorous and need to be pruned heavily. Will need staking and support.	Late in cooler areas				Scored well in the Digger's Seeds tomato taste test, 1993.
Kotlas	Medium-sized to large, red.	Pruning is not recommended but it should be well staked.	Early Short-summer seasons		6	Excellent Sweet	Slightly cold tolerant.
KY1	Flattened and slightly ribbed.	Rounded bushes that don't need support.	Early			Wonderful full flavour	Bred for commercial production in the Goulburn Valley, Vic. Very suited to inland areas but will also grow in cool climates. Resistant to fusarium and verticillium and could be used as rootstocks.
Latvian	Large (weighing up to 1 kg/2 lb).	Tall growing.	Mid to late			Good	
Longkeeper	Pale golden orange that can be picked when semi-ripe.	Vigorous vines that need support.					Long-life tomato that was found growing in a home garden. Fruit will store up to 3 months. Suited to cold climates.

Chart 1 (continued)

Name	Description	Plant	Season	Use	Taste	Notes
Lutschistzurich	Medium-sized, juicy, round and red.	Abundant cropper.	Early		Excellent	
Mama's Delight	Round and red.	Grows easily in the ground or in pots without being staked. Bountiful crop.		Good for drying and preserving.		A tomato for lazy gardeners.
Mama Mia	Oblong with slightly dry texture.			Drying, preserving, mixing into salads and making sauces.	Delicious	A hybrid marketed by the Floriana Co, Vic.
Manalucie	Yellow.	Bush type.	Late			First grown in Rockhampton, Qld in the 1930s. Grows in warm and cool areas (popular in NSW and Qld). Resists bacterial speck and fusarium wilt.
Mande	Medium to large, red.	Tall growing.			Medium	Grow well in outdoor gardens as well as inside glasshouses.
Marzano Lampadina	Meaty and elongated.	Bush type.		Good for making sauce or paste and can be dried.		Italian variety.
Mighty Red	Large and globe-shaped.	Vigorous plants.			Tasty	A hybrid plant popular with home gardeners. It is resistant to tobacco mosaic virus, fusarium wilt, grey leaf spot and some species of nematodes. A good rootstock plant.
Mikado	Large and purpley red.	Tall growing.	Early			A Seed Savers' Network cultivar.

Chart 1 (continued)

Cultivar/ Variety	Description		Season (early, mid, late)	Special Uses	Taste		Comments
	Fruit	Plant			Digger's Seeds Ranking	Author & Home Gardeners	
Moneymaker	Round red to scarlet. 10 cm (4 in) diameter.	Heavy crops—large clusters of up to 18 fruit.				Mild	A commercially bred bush tomato used for glasshouse production. Also grows well in open beds.
Moonshot	Round and smooth.	Vigorous, medium-sized and crops well over a long period.		Used in salads and for cooking.		Excellent	A well-known hybrid.
Mortgage Lifter	'Beefsteak'-type. Will grow to 2 kg (4½ lb) or more.					Delicious	For gardeners wanting to show off their prowess.
Napoli	Oblong or egg-shaped.	Bushy and bears plenty of fruit (more than the prolific-bearing 'Roma').	Early	For bottling, making sauce, for pizzas and for eating raw.			Verticillium resistant.
Nepal	Smooth, red and round.	Tall growing.	Late			Good	Suited to Tas. climate. Tolerates cool weather.
Oxheart	Shaped like a giant heart, hence the name.	Vigorous and tall. Good for growing in containers but sometimes a shy bearer.		'Meaty' tomato great for baking or stuffing. Excellent for bottling or cooking with.		Great Mild	
Peruvian Currant	Clusters of very small fruit.				26	Very tasty to excellent	Wild type, suitable for use as a rootstock for grafting onto.
Peruvian Sugarlump	Small and round.	Strong growing and produces throughout the year.			8	Very tasty	Ranked 8 in the Digger's Seed tomato test, 1993.

Chart 1 (continued)

Variety	Description	Growth habit	Use	No.	Flavour	Notes
Pixie	Small. Dwarfed plant.	Bushy. Ideal for pots as it only grows to about 60 cm (2 ft) tall.			Excellent	Plant could be pot grown inside a well lit house.
Ponderosa	Pinky red, flattened with a scalloped edge.	Strong grower but fairly sparse crop.	Great for putting on toast.		Tasty	An old variety available through the Seed Savers' Network.
Principe Borghese	Small, red and oval-shaped.	Prolific bearer.	Would respond well to drying.	24	Improved with drying.	An ancient heirloom cultivar from Italy.
Purple Calabash	Medium-sized and purplish. They ripen very quickly.	Medium to large.	Ideal for giving colour to salads. The flavour diminishes when the fruit is overripe.	18	Delicate Tasty	Don't be put off by the colour.
Redback	Firm, round and deep red.	Prolific bearer.	Salads and in cooking.		Old-fashioned flavour of heritage types	
Red Cloud	Small, slightly round with red skin and flesh.	Determinate growth habit.			Good	
Red Peach	Plum-sized and peach-coloured. Rough, almost scaly skin.	Strong growing.	Fresh, salad, drying.	13	Superb	Unusually sand-paper-like pink skin.
Roma	Thick, tough skin with almost no seeds. Teardrop-shaped.	Low-growing bush producing continuous crops.	Bottling, making paste and eating raw. OK for drying.	21	Acidic but strong	Resistant to fungal wilts and cracking. Slightly cold tolerant. Several seedling variations are found in home gardens.

Chart 1 (continued)

Cultivar/ Variety	Description — Fruit	Description — Plant	Season (early, mid, late)	Special Uses	Taste — Digger's Seeds Ranking	Taste — Author & Home Gardeners	Comments
Roma Nova	Thick, tough skin with almost no seeds. Teardrop-shaped.	Larger crops than 'Roma'.		Bottling, making paste and eating raw. OK for drying.		Acidic but strong	'Roma' type that has been improved to be tolerant to verticillium and fusarium wilt.
Rouge de Marmande	Large, flattened and ribbed. Very few seeds.	Vigorous. Needs to be staked.		Salad, cooking, sauce.		Great	Cold tolerant. An old-fashioned cultivar. Very popular staking variety.
Rutgers	Medium-sized, round and 'meaty'. Low in acid.	Bush forming. High yield.	Late	Good for bottling or eating straight from the bush.			Bred by Campbell's soup company in about 1928.
San Marzano	Deep red, elongated and teardrop-shaped. Medium-sized.	Bushy. Can be staked if necessary.		Paste, cooking and making sauces. Drying.		Great	
Saucy Sue		Bush type so needs no pruning.		Ideal for sauces.			
Scorpio		Vigorous. Needs staking or support.				Tasty	Resistant to bacterial wilt. Was bred especially for tropical areas.
Scotland Yellow	Smallish.			Salad, drying.	23	Great	Better taste than most red-skinned tomato fruits.
Sherry's Sweet Italian	Capsicum-like.	Bush forming.		'Meaty' bottling variety. Good for salads and stuffing.			

Chart 1 (continued)

Name	Fruit	Plant / Growth	Season	Uses	Score	Taste	Comments
Shimmeig Craig	Beautiful looking: yellow with pink streaks. Dryish flesh.	Leaves unusual: grey and hairy.			25		Shimmeig craig is Manx for 'striped rock'. Named by Tom Wagner in honour of his father who was the last person to speak the manx language.
Simpson's Summer Palace	Medium-sized, red and round.	Will grow to 2 m (6½ ft). May require staking.					Old heritage variety.
Striped German	Large with orange skin and mottled yellow flesh.					Very sweet	An outstanding cultivar.
Stuffing Mix				Ideal for stuffing. Good for sauce making.	'Shimmeig Stoo' scored 25	Great	All three varieties store well. Made up from Green Bell Pepper, Costoluto Genovense, Shimmeig Stoo.
Stupice	Medium-sized and plum-shaped.		Early— within 7 to 8 weeks		5		Obtained from Czechoslovakia. Good for cool areas.
Summertaste			Early				Produced by Qld Dept of Primary Industries for resistance to disease in warm-climate areas. Suitable for hot humid conditions. Could be used as a rootstock plant for grafting onto.
Sunrise	Bright orange cherry tomato.	Tall growing.		Salads, fresh.			Interesting colour.
Sunshine Girl	Golden and about the size of bantam eggs.	Continuous producer.		Salads	20	Excellent	
Super prize	Large and fleshy.	Small growing with good crop. Ideal for pots.				Good	

Chart 1 (continued)

122

Cultivar/ Variety	Description		Season (early, mid, late)	Special Uses	Taste		Comments
	Fruit	Plant			Digger's Seeds Ranking	Author & Home Gardeners	
Sweet 100	Tiny.	Tall growing and prolific bearer.		Taste wonderful if ripened on the vine. High vitamin C content. Drying.		Excellent and best tasting of all cherry tomatoes	Home gardeners might like to trial as a rootstock.
Sweetbite see 'Sweet 100'							
Sweetie	Cherry-red.	Vigorous, spreading vine, ideal for growing as espalier. Fruit hangs in bunches of 20 or more.		Salad, drying.		Great	
Tatura Dwarf Globe	Ribbed and flattened. Juicy.	Bushy dwarf.	Early	Excellent for making sauce.			Developed as a canning tomato. Could be grown in pots.
Thompson's Seedless Grape	Small, grape-sized and greenish yellow.	Bunches of fruit on a vigorous vine.		Salad.			
Tigerella	Small and green, with a yellow fleck.	Heavy yielding.		Outstanding for salads. Bite sized.		Tangy	
Tiny Tim	2 cm (1 in) diameter.	Hardy dwarf suitable for pots, hanging baskets and containers.		Wonderful in salads.		Great	Suitable for all climatic regions in Australia. It will grow through the wet season in the Qld tropics.
Tommy Toe	Small with a slightly mealy texture.	Not a big producer.			1	Average	Extremely resistant to diseases until time of first frosts. May be used as a rootstock plant.

Variety	Description	Plant	Season	Uses		Tasty	Notes
Tropic	Round and red.						Hybrid verticillium and fusarium resistant.
Verna Orange	Huge, heart-shaped and orange.	Long producer.	Early	'Meaty' flesh good for sandwiches (doesn't go mushy). Flavour diminishes if overripe.	28		
Vivian	Small to medium size.	Need staking. Suitable for greenhouses.		Salad, fresh.	7		An F₁ hybrid worth growing for old-fashioned tomato taste. Could be used as a rootstock for grafting as it is resistant to all wilts and root knot nematode.
Walter	Large, round and red with tough skin.	Large and bushy.					Resistant to some soil-borne diseases.
White Beauty	Novelty fruit with ivory-white skin. Medium size, high sugar content and few seeds.	Tall growing.		Good for slicing and using in salads.		Good	
World's Largest	Huge.	Tall growing.					Mainly grown as a novelty plant. Supposedly the biggest variety available. Try it and see if you can beat the record weight (3½ kg/ 7½ lb) for the world's largest tomato.
Yellow	Large, round and yellow, with smooth skin. Low in acid.			Salads, cooking and preserving.			
Yellow Baby	Medium-sized, yellow and pear-shaped.			Often used in salad cocktails.		Good	An ornamental type.
Yellowboy	Small, egg-shaped and lemon-coloured.	Vigorous and needs staking.					

Chart I (continued)

Cultivar/ Variety	Description		Season (early, mid, late)	Special Uses	Taste		Comments
	Fruit	Plant			Digger's Seeds Ranking	Author & Home Gardeners	
Yellow Cherry Cocktail	Exactly like 'Red Cherry Cocktail' except yellow instead of red.			Favoured by restaurants for use in salads or for plate decoration.			
Yellow Delicious	A startling bright yellow, but remains a deep emerald green until ripening begins, creating a vivid colour scheme.					Better than most red-skinned types	Released in 1994 by Digger's Seeds.
Yellow Pear	Golden, pear-shaped with a glossy sheen. Form in clusters and range in size from thumb size to 5 or 6 cm (2–2¹/₂ in). Acid free.	A tall vigorous vine.		Used whole in salads. Also in pies, jam, for bottling and drying, or being crystalised.			First recorded as being grown in 1884. Seems to be resistant to leaf blight.
Yellow Plum	Same characteristics as 'Roma', except yellow instead.	Similar to 'Roma' but vine more vigorous. Good for pots and containers.		Bottling, drying, sauce, paste.			
Yugoslav	Huge and pink with a pointed top end.	Tall growing.					Available from WA. Brought to Australia by people from the former Yugoslav Republic.
Wild Cuatomate	Very tiny.			Drying, salads.		Strongly flavoured Wonderful taste	Probably one of the truly wild tomatoes. Seedlings may be used as rootstocks.
Wild Red Currant	Tiny (3–4 g/¹/₁₀ oz). Ripen sequentially. Produced on trusses.	Indeterminate growth habit. Needs staking.		Salad, drying.		Sweet to acid	A species tomato— *Lycopersicon pimpinellifolium*. Could be used as a rootstock.

2: The Seed Savers' Network Top Tomato Selection

Selecting the right tomato to grow is an important decision for most home gardeners, and involves searching for plant characteristics suitable for their particular use. The following tomatoes are some favourites of Michael and Jude Fanton of the Seed Savers' Network in Byron Bay.

All the tomato seeds available through the Seed Savers' Network have records on source and availability. Catalogue numbers for filing and easy access to the source of those varieties are included in the chart. The network has been sending out regular seedlists and newsletters to members since 1985.

Purple Calabash

Oxheart

Grosse Lisse

Chart 2: The Seed Savers' Network Top Tomato Selection

| Cultivar/ Variety | Description | | Season (early, mid, late) | Special Uses | Taste | Comments |
	Fruit	Plant				
Ailsa Craig 1291	— See other list for extra information —					Of Scottish origin, this tomato is named after an island in the Firth of Clyde. One of the most popular varieties in the UK. Great for cool areas.
Beaudesert Oxheart 538	Large fruits.	Large and spreading. Can be pruned back to lower shoots and will produce a second crop.	Will grow in winter in mild-climate areas			
Best of Bonn 486	Red and golfball-sized. Slighly ridged, flattened with a soft skin.	Vine-like.			Very tasty	Similar to 'Bonner's Best'.
Big Boy 243	Medium to large, spherical and red.	Vigorous, growing to 4 m (13 ft).	Early			Produces well in the Castlemaine area of Vic.
Budiar 485	Deep red, round and medium-sized.	Grows to 2 m (6½ ft). Leaves are potato type.				Wilt resistant and will tolerate drought conditions.
Burbank 885	Red.	A very productive bush with a determinate growth habit. Produces simultaneously ripening fruit.	Early		Very tasty	Will fruit over a long period in Qld.
Centennial 190	Egg-sized.					Originally obtained from NZ.
Cherry Pratt 137	Cherry-sized.	Bears well and has indeterminate growth habit.				The seed came from Murwillumbah, Qld. The plant seems tolerant of wet conditions.

Chart 2 (continued)

Defender 2235	Round and fleshy with thick walls.	Can be grown successfully in pots.				Grown in the south of France successfully during winter. Cold tolerant.
Deutcher Fleiss 162					Good	Thrives in Canberra.
Goed Currant 2206	Very small (1 cm/½ in) and grape-like.	Large and bushy. Huge producer and crops over a long period. Berries do not drop from plant when ripe.			Great taste	
Graf Zeppelin 366	Golfball-sized.	Has a climbing habit and has been known to suppress couch grass.	Early		Very tasty	Sensitive to frost and intolerant of wet soils. Survives in hot climatic zones.
Grosse Lisse 0260	Red, round with smooth skin. Soft and juicy.		Some plants have fruited into July, despite nearby frosts		Lovely	One of the first varieties of its type, exists in many forms and is still available today. Originally grown by a market gardener in Camberwell, Vic., in the 1930s.
Grosse Rot 367	Large, red and firm.					From Bacchus Marsh in Vic. 'Grosse Rot' means 'big red' in German.
Hawkesbury College 1599	Large and red.	Vigorous.		All	Good taste	Developed by the Hawkesbury College, NSW, about 50 years ago and now no longer commercially available.
Isabella 675	Medium-sized.	Tall growing. Needs staking. Performs well in glasshouses.			Very tasty	Of Dutch origin.

Chart 2 (continued)

Cultivar/ Variety	Description		Season (early, mid, late)	Special Uses	Taste	Comments
	Fruit	Plant				
Italian Plum 410	Red and globular.	Indeterminate growth habit and very wide leaf. A heavy, consistent cropper.			Good	Disease resistant. Suitable for rootstock.
Latvian 191	Large, fleshy and pink.					Easily diseased in some areas.
Maltese 1390	Similar to 'Roma'. Squarish.	Vine-like.		Just the right size for slicing and placing on crackers for a quick snack.		
Manalucie 249	Golden, golfball-sized and slightly acidic.	Bears very heavy crops for about 2 months in warm areas, but will produce continuous crops in cooler areas. Strong growing with indeterminate growth habit.	Early		Very tasty	Popular in SE Qld. Fairly tolerant of pests and diseases.
Nadja 268	Small and juicy.	Leaves are potato-like and growth is indeterminate.	Early and bears continuously until the first frosts		Good	A selection from the Hungarian Institute of Agrobotany.
Oxheart 130	——— See other list for extra information ———					A very popular variety. Seeds were sent by a SSN subscriber in Lowood, Qld.
Paprika 2314	Hollow, yellow and look like a capsicum.	Tall and will need staking.		Stuffing-type tomato. Can be used for pickles.		Originally obtained from Yugoslavia. Frost tolerant.

Chart 2 (continued)

Peruvian Bush Cherry 870	Cherry-sized.	Strong-growing vine. Bears continuously. Very hardy.				Grows well in Casuarina, NT, where few other tomatoes will survive.
Phelp's Yellow 1592	Thin-skinned with few seeds.			Very tasty raw. Go to pulp once cooked. Can be used in soups, for pastes and for purees.		
Pink Ponderosa 353	Tough stems. Large and pink (up to 500 g/1 lb). Similar to 'Oxheart'. Low in acid.	Strong with indeterminate growth reaching 2 m (6½ ft). Produces extremely well on the lower part of the plant.	Plant in winter in northern climates			Seems to lack in taste when grown in the Sydney area but performs well in cooler areas. The fruit are susceptible to sun scald and fruit fly attack. Does not store well because of the soft, easily bruised skin.
Potato Leaf 475	Medium-sized and rich red.	Vigorous and produces fruit continually for 6 months.				Pest and disease tolerant. Will withstand hot and cool climate variations and is recommended for southern parts of Australia.
Purple Calabash 536	Medium-sized, very fluted and a pronounced purple when ripe.	Vigorous and can be staked. Will crop continuously for 3 months.			Strong	Shows tolerance to heat and pests and diseases.
Red Chief 1292	Good size. More flesh than most.				Excellent	Originally available through Anderson's seeds.
Red Cloud 2239	Firm, deep red and juicy. Medium size.	Usually gives one good crop. Will not overwinter in cool-climate areas. Big producer. A staking variety.			Good	

Chart 2 (continued)

Cultivar/ Variety	Description		Season (early, mid, late)	Special Uses	Taste	Comments
	Fruit	Plant				
Red Colossus 037	Large (about 750 g/ 1½ lb).	Indeterminate, vigorous growth and a prolific bearer.				Can be grown from the York Peninsula to central Qld coastal areas.
Red Ponderosa 322	Very large, flattened and ridged.	Indeterminate growth.		Sandwiches, fresh.	Tasty	Can be cropped in northern Qld.
Small Yellow 161	Yellow and spherical, about 2½ cm (1 in) across.			Salads.		Seems pest and disease resistant when grown in SA.
Stowers Money Maker 673	Small to medium.	Tall. Needs staking.				A very old type grown by a Seed Savers' Network subscriber in Tas.
Schneider 1288	Small, red and pear-shaped.	Vine-like growth.	Fruit production usually from Jan. to June		Good	
Winter White 2027	Vary in size. White.	Soft, intolerant of cold conditions.			Good	
Yellow Egg 953	Small and egg-shaped. Will ripen months after picking if picked green and mature.	A staking variety with very vigorous growth, resistant to extreme weather conditions.				One gardener in Minlaton, SA, picked 40 kg (90 lb) from one plant over a 6-month period.
Yellow Kralowa 232	Medium-sized (5–8 cm/2–3 in diameter) and yellow.	Usually staked. Produces large clusters over an extended period.	Early			
Yellow Pear 352	Low in acid.	Vine-like with a leafy profile, producing fruit in bunches. Sends down roots from prostrate stems to give extra root power. Very hardy.		Salads (colour).		Grows well in NT—right into the wet season.
Yugoslavian	Large.	Lots of leaves. Good			Medium	Seed originally obtained

Useful Addresses

Seed Suppliers

*Bay Seed Garden (organic seeds)
PO Box 1164,
Busselton WA 6280.
Tel (097) 52 2513.

**Biodynamic Gardeners' Association
Seedbank**, Vic.
c/o 15 Dionne St,
Doncaster East Vic. 3109.
For enquiries send a SSAE.

Brisbane Organic Growers Inc. (BOG)
34 Heaton St,
Rocklea Qld 4106.
Tel (07) 277 1507.

Broerson Seed & Bulbs
c/o Silvan
Silvan Vic. 3795.
Tel (03) 9737 9202, Fax (03) 9737 9707.

*Digger's Seeds
[105 Latrobe Pde] PO Box 3000,
Dromana Vic. 3936.
Tel (059) 871877, Fax (059) 81 4298

*Eden Seeds
MS 316
Gympie Qld 4570.
For enquiries send a SSAE.

Fairbank's Selected Seeds
542 Footscray Rd
Footscray Vic. 3011.
Tel (03) 9689 4500, Fax (03) 9687 7089.

Goodman Seeds
PO Box 91
Bairnsdale Vic. 3875.
Tel (051) 52 4024.

Greenpatch Organic Seeds
PO Box 1285,
Taree NSW 2430.
Tel (02) 6550 7327.

Henderson's Seeds
165 Templestowe Rd,
Lower Templestowe Vic. 3107.
Tel (03) 9850 2266, Fax (03) 9850 6794.

*Heritage Seed Collection
'Wombat Bluff',
W Tree,
via Buchan Vic. 3885.
Tel (051) 55 0227, (051) 53 1034.

Mr. Fothergill's Seeds
22 Prime Dve,
Seven Hills NSW 2147.
Tel (02) 9838 0500, Fax (02) 9838 7748.

*New Gippsland Seed Farm
PO Box 1,
Silvan Vic. 3795.
Tel (03) 9737 9560, Fax (03) 9737 9292.

*Phoenix Seeds
PO Box 207,
Snug Tas. 7044.
Tel (002) 67 9592, Fax (002) 679 592.

*Potager Seeds
PO Box 5089,
Alphington Vic. 3078.
For enquiries send a SSAE.

*Seed Savers' Network
PO Box 975,
Byron Bay NSW 2481.
For enquiries send a SSAE.

* = suppliers that sell heritage seeds
SSAE = stamped self-addressed envelope

Yates Seeds
Arthur Yates & Co.,
PO Box 4072,
Milperra NSW 2214.
Tel (02) 9771 2911.

Suppliers of Fertilisers

Arthur Yates and Co.
PO Box 4072,
Milperra NSW 2214.
Tel (02) 9771 2911, Fax (02) 9774 5177.
Organic mix fertilisers and mulch and
general garden products, available at most
plant nurseries.

Botanical Distribution
Factory 8, 2-10 Hallam Rd,
Hallam Vic. 3803.
Tel (03) 9703 2900, Fax (03) 9703 2899.
Supply 'Black Gold' compost and Seasol
liquid seaweed products.

Debco
12 McKirdys Rd,
Tyabb Vic. 3913.
Tel (059) 77 4755, Fax (059) 77 4921.
Supply soils, composts, coprapeat,
Phostrogen fertiliser, available at most
plant nurseries.

Galloping Garden
PO Box 1,
Tally Ho Vic. 3149.
Tel (018) 03 3723.
Organic fertiliser pellets, available from
most plant nurseries.

Grow Better Organic Fertiliser
5 Diligent Dr,
Bayswater North Vic. 3153.
Tel (03) 9720 7475, Fax (03) 9720 7429.

Neutrog
Mines Rd,
Kanmantoo SA 5252.
Tel (085) 38 5077.
Supply Neutrog organic fertilisers and
other plant food products.

Pivot, Head Office,
160 Queen St,
Melbourne Vic. 3000.
Tel (03) 9605 0400.

Supply organic blood and bone and Pivot
fertiliser range, available from selected
plant nurseries and Pivot country depots.

Seaminerals
Couger St,
Adelaide SA 5000.
Fax (08) 2121533.

Vicmill Products
23 Railway St,
Euroa Vic. 3666,
Tel (03) 5795 2090, Fax (03) 5795 1055.

*Suppliers of Liquid Seaweed and
Fish Products*

Gerhard Grasser
RSD Sunday Rd,
Callignee Vic. 3844.
Tel/Fax (051) 95 5396.
Seagrow products (seaweed products
including Natrakelp).

Multicrop (Aust.)
926 Mountain Hwy,
Bayswater Vic. 3153.
Tel (03) 9720 2200.
or 47 Kambora Ave,
Davidson NSW 2085.
Multicrop products, Maxicrop and
Multiguard snail and slug pellets.

Natrakelp
20-24 Enterprise St,
Maroochydore Qld 4558.
Tel (07) 5445 5054, Free Call (008) 67 2174.
Fax (07) 5445 5499.
Natrakelp.

**North Coast Biodynamic Farming and
Gardening Association of Australia**
48 Glenniffer Rd,
Bonville NSW 2441.
Tel (066) 53 4449.
Biodynamic Fish Emulsion.

Sunstate Sea Products
PO Box 1367,
Bundaburg Qld 4670.
Tel. (071) 52 1133.
Bundaburg Marine Fish Emulsion.

Suppliers of Worms

Contact a worm farmer in your state.

Australian Worm Growers' Association
58 Derham St,
Port Melbourne Vic. 3207.
Publicity office
Ms Jean Steele
Worm CD
47 Carrawa Dve
Boronia Vic. 3155.
Tel (03) 9762 8817, Fax (03) 9761 1728.

Mini-Greenhouses

Fertool Industries
97 Abbot Rd,
Hallam Vic. 3803.
Tel (03) 9796 4433.
Suncell bubble plastic teepee (Suncell Plant Guard) and horticultural products.

Suntech Technology
PO Box 4141,
Knox City Centre Vic. 3152.
Tel (03) 9887 4888, Mobile (015) 52 7727,
Fax (03) 9887 1999.
Hydronurture water-filled cellular mini-greenhouses (teepee shaped).

Yates
PO Box 4072,
Milperra NSW 2214.
Tel (02) 9771 2911, Fax (02) 9774 5177.
Mini-greenhouses for seedlings.

Suppliers of Biological Pest, Disease and Weed Control Materials

Amgrow
Head Office,
358 Castlereagh Rd,
Penrith NSW 2750.
Tel (047) 29 0470, Fax (047) 29 1318.
Snail deterrent.

Biological Services
PO Box 501,
Loxton SA 5333.
Tel (08) 8584 6977, Fax (08) 8584 5057.
Predators for two-spotted mite, moths and white fly.

Bioprotection
PO Box 35,
Warwick Qld 4370.
Tel. (076) 66 1592, Fax (076) 66 1639.
Predator mites for control of two-spotted mite and trichogramma wasps for control of heliothis moths.

Botanical Distribution
Factory 8, 2-10 Hallam Rd,
Hallam Vic. 3803
Ezi-mulch (recycled wool product).
Tel (03) 9703 2900, Fax (03) 9703 2899.

Bugs for Bugs
28 Orton Street,
Mundubbera Qld 4626.
Tel (071) 65 4663, Fax (071) 65 4626.

Dunluce International
PO Box 922,
Killara St Ives NSW 2075
Tel/Fax (02) 9983 1776.
Sticky traps and codlin moth traps, cockroach traps, barrier glue (Trappit and Magnet products).

Environmental and Revegetation Products
PO Box 218,
Mentone Vic. 3194.
Tel (03) 9558 1070, Fax (03) 9558 0505.
Weed-control mats (biodegradable); one free weed mat sample available on request.

Hawkesbury Integrated Pest Management Service
PO Box 436,
Richmond NSW 2753.
Tel (045) 70 1331, Fax (045) 70 1314.
Predator mites.

Multicube (a division of R.J. & R.C. Investments)
Rob and Rhonda Riddell,
'Warrawee' Gulf Rd,
Yarra Glen Vic. 3775.
Tel (03) 9730 1660, Fax (03) 9730 1610.
Grow & Mulch Cubes for weed control and mulching.

Neemoil Australia
PO Box 99,
South Lismore NSW 2480.

Tel (066) 291057.
Neem oil extract.

Silo Horticulture
PO Box 16,
St Kilda Vic 3182.
Tel (03) 9534 9441.
Ladybirds (eggs) to eat spider mite or
aphids.

Gardening Organisations

Australasian Biological Control Inc.
PO Box 436 Bourke St,
Richmond NSW 2753.
Tel (045) 70 1331, Fax (045) 70 1314.

**Biodynamic Gardeners' Association and
Biodynamic Resource Centre**
PO Box 479,
Leongatha Vic. 3953.
Please send a SSAE for enquiries.

**Bio-Dynamic Farming & Gardening
Association**
Fax (066) 55 8551.
Telephone staffed by volunteer workers.
Coffs Regional Organic
Producers Organisation
PO Box 363
Coffs Harbour NSW 2450

Garden Club Of Australia
H. Atherton
50 Lochlan St
Thirroul NSW 2515.
Tel/Fax (042) 67 1181.
For enquiries send a SSAE.

Henry Doubleday Research Association
816 Comleroy Rd,
Kurrajong NSW 2758.
Send a SSAE for any enquiries.

**Householders Options to Protect the
Environment (HOPE)**
RMB,
Mansfield Vic. 3722.
Tel (057) 75 2988.

Heritage Seed Collection (HSC)
c/o W Tree,
via Buchan Vic. 3885.
Tel (051) 55 0227 or (051) 53 1034.

**Organic Retailers & Growers Association
of Australia (ORGAA)**
PO Box 12852 A'Beckett St,
Melbourne Vic. 3000.
Tel. (03) 9737 9799.
Home gardeners can become associate
members and obtain a listing of member
retail stores selling organic produce.

**National Association for Sustainable
Agriculture in Australia (NASSA)**
PO Box 768,
Stirling SA 5152.
Tel (08) 8370 8455, Fax (08) 8370 8381.
National standards booklet available
listing registered products used for organic
gardening and farming.

Soil Association of South Australia
PO Box 2497,
Adelaide SA 5001.
For enquiries send a SSAE.

**Willing Workers on Organic Farms
(WWOOF)**
c/o W Tree,
via Buchan Vic 3885.
Tel (051) 55 0227 or (051) 53 1034.

Publications

Acres Australia
PO Box 27,
Eumundi Qld 4562.
Tel (074) 491881, Fax (074) 491889.
Subscription magazine published six times
per year.

Earth Garden
RMB 427,
Trentham Vic. 3458.
Fax (054) 241743.
For enquiries send a SSAE.

Grass Roots
Night Owl Publications
PO Box 242,
Euroa Vic. 3666.
Tel (03) 5794 7263.

Permaculture International
PO Box 1,
Tyalgum NSW 2484.

Journal published four times per year available from newsagents. For enquiries please send a SSAE.
Tel (066) 22 0020, Fax (066) 22 0579.

Soft Technology
247 Flinders La.,
Melbourne Vic. 3000.
Tel (03) 9650 3623, Fax (03) 9650 4175.

Published quarterly by the Alternative Technology Association, available from newsagents.

The Organic Farmer
c/o ORGAA
PO Box 12852 A'Beckett St,
Melbourne Vic. 3000.
Tel (03) 9386 2999.

Bibliography

Arthur Yates and Co. (1992) *Yates Garden Guide* (revised edition), HarperCollins [Angus & Robertson], Pymble, New South Wales.

Australasian Biological Control (1995) *The Good Bug Book*, Australasian Biological Control Inc. Queensland.

Baker, K. F. (1957) *The UC* [University of California] *System for Producing Healthy Container-Grown Plants Through the Use of Clean Soil, Clean Stock and Sanitation*, University of California, Berkeley, California.

Ballinger, R. & Swaan, H. (1982) *Vegetable Gardening In South-Eastern Australia*, Caxton Press, Christchurch, New Zealand.

Bartholomew, M. (1981) *Square Foot Gardening*, Rodale Press, Emmaus, Pennsylvania.

Bennett, P. (1989) *Australia and New Zealand Organic Gardening* (revised edition), Child & Associates, Frenchs Forest, New South Wales.

Blanchard, D. (1992) *A Colour Atlas of Tomato Diseases*, Wolfe Publications Ltd.

Blazey, C. (1994) *The Digger's Club Guide to Gardening Success* Doubleday, Transworld, Moonbank, New South Wales.

Brooks, J. (1984) *The Garden Book*, Crown Publishers, New York.

Bubel, N. (1978) *The Seed Starters' Handbook*, Rodale Press, Emmaus, Pennsylvania.

Clarke, G. & Toogood, A. (1992) *The Complete Book of Plant Propagation*, Ward Lock, London.

Clayton, S. (1994) *The Reverse Garbage Mulch Book*, Hyland House, Melbourne.

Creasy, R. (1982) *The Complete Book of Edible Landscaping*, Sierra Book Club, California.

Davies, R. (1991) *Your Garden Questions Answered*, Hyland House, Melbourne.

de Vaus, P. (1988) *Vegetables for Small Gardens and Containers*, Hyland House, Melbourne.

Dean, Esther (1977) *Esther Dean's Gardening Book: Growing Without Digging*, Harper Row, Australia.

Department of Agriculture New South Wales (1981) *The Home Vegetable Garden*, Department of Agriculture, New South Wales.

Edmanson, J. (1992) *Jane Edmanson's Working Manual For Gardeners*, Lothian, Port Melbourne.

Fanton, M. & J. (1993) *The Seed Savers' Handbook*, Seed Savers' Network, Byron Bay, New South Wales.

Fowler, C. & Mooney, P. (1990) *Shattering-Food, Politics, and the Loss of Genetic Diversity*, University of Arizona Tucson Press, USA.

French, J. (1990) *Natural Control of Garden Pests*, Aird Books, Flemington, Victoria.

French, J. (1991) *Jackie French's Guide to Companion Planting*, Aird Books, Flemington, Victoria.

French, J. (1995) *Jackie French's Top Ten Vegetables*, Aird Books, Flemington, Victoria.

Fullelove, G. (1992) *Tomato Pests and Diseases and Disorders*, Qld. Dept. of Primary Industries.

Fulton, M. (1983) *Encyclopedia of Food & Cookery*, Octopus Books, Sydney.

Garner, R. J. (1947) *The Grafter's Handbook*, Cassell Publishers, London.

Garzoli, K. (1990) *Greenhouses* (reprint) Australian Government Publishing Service, Canberra.

Gilbert, A. L. (1991) *Yates Green Guide To Gardening: A No Fuss Guide to Organic Gardening*, HarperCollins [Angus & Robertson], North Ryde, New South Wales.

Gilbert, A. L. (1992) *No Garbage: Composting and Recycling*, Lothian, Melbourne.

Hamilton, G. (1987) *Successful Organic Gardening*, Macmillan, South Melbourne, Victoria.

Handreck, K. (1993) *Gardening Down Under*, CSIRO Publications, East Melbourne, Victoria.

Hely, P. C., Pasfield, G. & Gellatley, J. G. (1982) *Insect Pests of Fruit and Vegetables in New South Wales*, Inkata Press, Melbourne.

Herd, M. (ed.) (1991) *The Comprehensive Guide: Brunning's Australian Gardener* HarperCollins [Angus & Robertson], North Ryde, New South Wales.

Hessayon, Dr D. G. (1985) *The Vegetable Expert*, pbi Publications, Waltham Cross, Hertfordshire.

Hodges, J. (ed.) (1995) *The Natural Gardener: A Complete Guide to Organic Gardening*, HarperCollins [Angus & Robertson], Pymble, New South Wales.

Hudson, R. L. (1982) *Organic Gardening In New Zealand*, Reed Methuen, Auckland.

Jones, J. B. & Jones, J. P. (1992) *Compendium of Tomato Diseases* APS Press USA.

Katzen, M. (1977) *Moosewood Cookbook*, Ten Speed Press, Berkley, California.

Katzen, M. (1982) *The Enchanted Broccoli Forest*, Ten Speed Press, Berkley, California.

Kinsella, M. & Martindale, W. L. (1976) *Vegetables in the Home Garden* (tenth edition) Department of Agriculture, Victoria.

Krone, B. & Harris, W. H., Bulletin No. 26 (booklet), *Tomato Culture in Victoria* (fifth edition), Department of Agriculture, Victoria.

Larkom, J. (1991) *Oriental Vegetables: The Complete Guide for Garden and Kitchen*, John Murray, London.

Mastalerz, J. W. (ed.) (1976) *Bedding Plants*, Pennsylvania Flower Growers, Pennsylvania.

May, M. (ed.) (1977) *All About Tomatoes*, Ortho Books, San Francisco, California.

McMaugh, J. (1985) *What Garden Pest or Disease is That?*, Lansdowne Press, Dee Why, New South Wales.

Mollison, B. (1991) *Introduction To Permaculture*, Tagari Publications, Tyalgum, New South Wales.

Murphy, D. (1993) *Earthworms In Australia*, Hyland House, Melbourne.

New Zealand Biodynamic Association (1989) *Biodynamics: New Directions for Farming and Gardening in New Zealand*, Random House, Albany, Auckland.

Poincelot, R. P. (1986) *Organic No-dig, No-weed Gardening: A Revolutionary Method for Easy Gardening*, Thorsons/Rodale, Northamptonshire.

Rickards, P. (ed.) (1988) *A Garden Programme for Everyone*, Association for the Blind, Brighton Beach, Victoria.

Riotte, L. (1975) *Carrots Love Tomatoes*, Garden Way Publishing, Charlotte, Vermont.

Roads, M. J. (1989) *The Natural Magic Of Mulch*, Greenhouse Publications, Richmond, Victoria.

Smith, K. & I. (1994) *The Aussie Tomato Book*, Viking O'Neil, Ringwood, Victoria.

Sturgen, J. (1993) *Gardening With Containers*, Viking O'Neil, Ringwood, Victoria.

Sunstrom, A. C. (1979) *Simple Hydroponics for Australian Home Gardeners*, Thomas Nelson, Melbourne.

Sutherland, S. (1996) *Hydroponics for Everyone* (revised edition), Hyland House, Melbourne.

Sutton & Sons (1884) *The Culture of Vegetables and Flowers from Seeds and Roots*, Hamilton Adams & Co., London.

The Electricity Council (1970) *Electric Growing*, The Electricity Council, London.

University of California (1982) *Publication 3274—Integrated Pest Management for Tomatoes*, USA.

Vilmorin-Andrieux, Mlle (1976) *The Vegetable Garden*, (English edition), Ten Speed Press, California.

Watson, W. (ed.) (1936) *The Gardener's Assistant*, vol. 1 to 6, Grensham Publishing, London.

Whealy, K. (1994) *Seed Savers' 1994 Yearbook*, Seed Savers' Exchange, Decorah, Iowa.

Williams, R. (ed.) (1992) *The Complete Book of Patio and Container Gardening*, Ward Lock, London.

Wright, J. I. (1983) *Plant Propagation for the Amateur Gardener*, Blandford Press, Poole.

Yepsen, R. B. Jr (ed.) (1966) *Organic Plant Protection*, Rodale Press, Emmaus, Pennsylvania.

Ziff Cool, J. (1994) *Tomatoes: A Country Garden Cook Book*, Collins, San Francisco, California.

Zola, N. & Gott, B. (1992) *Koorie Plants Koorie People*, The Koorie Heritage Trust, Melbourne.

Index

Entries in bold refer to photographs that appear on different pages from the text; entries in italics refer to drawings that appear on different pages from the text.